YOU SAY TOMATO
I SAY TOMATO

A SIMPLE GUIDE TO GROWING FLAVORFUL
TOMATOES IN VARYING CLIMATES FROM SEED
TO PRUNING, SUPPORTING, HARVESTING, AND
PRESERVING

Percy Sargeant

HIGHEST HILL PUBLISHING

Contents

"Seek roses in December – ice in June;
Hope constancy in wind, or corn in chaff;
Believe a woman or an epitaph,
Or any other thing that's false, before
You trust in critics, who themselves are sore"

Lord Byron 1778 - 1824

For my dear mother and father.
In life, we loved you dearly, in death we love you still.

Introduction

"The raw tomato, devoured in the garden when freshly picked, is a horn of abundance of simple sensations, a radiating rush in one's mouth that brings with it every pleasure...a tomato, an adventure." – Muriel Barbery

There are two wonderful experiences that can make anyone fall in love with tomatoes, known as gustatory memory and olfactory memory. These two memories are what kick in when you taste a delicious fresh tomato, and your mind is taken back to the pizza you had on holiday or the sauce your grandma used to make. No matter how hard you attempt to replicate the recipe, the senses fail to evoke those intense memories.

"When you eat a tomato, you want the adventure!"

I wanted the adventure, so I set on one. I had heard that "failures lead to success," but in my tomato-growing journey, I've experienced numerous failures, leading me to doubt the validity of this statement.

My failures weren't due to a lack of effort. In fact, I belonged to the group that extensively studied books and watched educational videos on achieving successful tomato growth.

And by the way, if you are thinking "He might have done the research but not taken actions accordingly", I would very much like to correct you. I belonged to the 2% of folks out there who implement what they learn.

And yes, I had the same question in my mind, you might be having right now.

Why did nothing seem to work?

Why didn't I get the flavorful healthy tomatoes that I wanted?

Despite my urge to give up, I kept trying, and, after a number of trials and errors and failures, I found the answers to my questions. And this book contains everything I learned the hard way.

But before you go ahead and gain the knowledge from the comfort of your room, ask yourself:

Why bother growing your own tomatoes?

Nowadays, a vast majority of people have no idea where their food comes from. They are unaware of where their food is grown and how it is processed. They have no clue what CHEMICALS are being used to grow the food they spend tons of their money on.

Besides, there has been a noted increase in the shortage of tomatoes. (olmedaorigenes, 2022). There are several reasons for this, some of which are political reasons influencing the supply of different edibles, including tomatoes. One of the reasons for the shortage of tomatoes is the climate change and the natural hazards affecting the production of tomatoes.

Inflation is acting as the cherry on the top and making it difficult for everyone to get healthy fresh tomatoes. For all these reasons, learning how to grow juicy, succulent, flavorful tomatoes of your own has become a need these days.

If you learn and master the art of growing tomatoes, things happening around the globe will not be able to affect your kitchen's supply of fresh tomatoes. Besides, you will have peace of mind knowing where your tomatoes are coming from.

The health benefits of the fresh homegrown tomatoes will leave you amazed and you will thank yourself for growing them. Nothing in terms of flavor, aroma, and nutritional value can compare a homegrown tomato with that you would buy in a store.

There are never-ending perks to homegrown tomatoes, and if you want to enjoy them all, this book is for you.

This book is not going to provide you with the superficial theoretical knowledge of how beautiful tomatoes are and how they are red in color and their leaves are a beautiful shade of green.

Instead, you will learn how you can get those healthy plants in your garden and witness the green little fruits turning into red healthy tomatoes.

You'll start with learning the basics, then you will go ahead and acquire understanding of the requirements for robust tomato plant health. You will then get well-versed in the suitable conditions for growing the juicy reds.

The chapters of this book are a step-by-step guide towards growing your succulent fruits. I'll walk you through the journey of planting a little seed and looking after it until it becomes a luscious plant.

But that's not it. There are a number of things that can go wrong. What about the pests and diseases that your plants might come across? Don't you worry! You will be learning to address them as well.

While providing you with the knowledge of steps to take to achieve your outcome, I'll guide you about the steps to avoid as well. In other words, you'll learn about the mistakes to avoid on this adventurous journey.

With initial hands-on experience as a novice tomato grower, I've accumulated years of expertise and research-supported insights. I can share valuable, lesser-known tips and tricks to enhance your tomato-growing journey. I have studied and practiced gardening various food crops for most of my life. In my experience, I have learned the gems I wish everyone to know about, and implement, in their home gardens.

Growing tomatoes is not a tough job but growing high-quality tomatoes rich in flavor and aroma is something very few people are capable of. This book will simply help you gain that knowledge to learn and master the skill of growing flavorful tomatoes successfully.

Interestingly enough, being a couch potato can be the biggest hindrance in growing tomatoes. Be ready to invest time in learning and applying knowledge, putting effort into properly caring for your tomato garden.

As you set on the journey, you will find times when you'll enjoy the process a lot whereas sometimes you will not feel like going in your garden. But remember it's about consistent effort and patience. If you are willing to put in consistent effort and be patient during the journey, this book is surely going to help you obtain your objective.

So, let's start the journey and discover the charm of growing tomatoes and experience their appetizing benefits.

You can download a free pdf of "21 diverse recipes from various cuisines worldwide that use TOMATOES in their ingredients"

https://bit.ly/43hUFt6

Chapter One

Appreciating the Humble Tomato

According to the 2021 statistics, the market showed that tomato consumption was at 37 million metric tons. That's the equivalent of around 4.9 million elephants! (Consumption: 2021 in the Wake of 2020 - Tomato News, n.d.)

This is a lot of tomatoes. Producing this large number of tomatoes to meet the needs of consumers is a huge task and is generally accomplished commercially by the use of some chemicals and genetically engineered seeds and seedlings of tomatoes.

When this huge fact dawned upon me years back, and I discovered the potential dangers of commercial tomatoes compared to the health benefits of homegrown tomatoes, I vowed never to buy another tomato again.

If you think I would give up on fresh salads and my favorite tomato sauce, you would be very wrong. So, I went with the only sensible and logical alternative, which was to grow my own tomatoes.

Yeah, my initial batches didn't even look anything close to tomatoes. But slowly, I got the results I wanted.

But before we get into the dos and don'ts of growing the plant, let's first get into the basics. Some of the topics we'll discuss in depth are the benefits of growing your own tomatoes, an overview of their types, and the basics of what tomatoes need.

WHAT EXACTLY IS A TOMATO?

Tomatoes have been on our kitchen counters and in our meals for a very long time, and it's almost impossible to imagine them growing in the wild. But there was a time when our ancestors used to forage for them in the wild.

Tomatoes have experienced centuries of cultivation and hybridization, undergoing significant changes in that period. Presently, there exist over 10,000 types of tomatoes. (A History of Tomatoes, n.d.) Many centuries ago, well before Europeans arrived in the New World, tomatoes thrived naturally in the Andes of western South America. The local people grew them and later took the plant northward through Central America into Mexico. In the early 16th century, when the Spanish arrived, they discovered the residents cultivating a food crop known as "tomato" in their native language.

Early explorers transported tomato seeds from Mexico to Spain. Subsequently, the plant was disseminated to Italy by the mid-1500s, where it started being integrated into local cuisine. In the ensuing years, tomato plants were grown across Europe, mainly for decorative purposes.

During its journey, the tomato had various names, such as wolf peach and gold apple. In France, it was labeled a love apple (pomme d'amour) and believed to have aphrodisiac qualities. Due to the misconception that the tomato was toxic, many referred to it as the "poison apple." (A History of Tomatoes, n.d.)

It is true that the foliage, branches, and roots of the tomato contain solanine, a neurotoxin, and should, therefore, not be consumed. Additionally, the tomato is a kind of deadly nightshade (Atropa belladonna).

The apparent evidence of the tomato's toxicity stemmed from a mistaken belief. Although it was accurate that affluent Europeans perished after eating tomatoes, the blame lay not with the tomato itself but with the pewter tableware utilized. The acidity in tomatoes extracted lead from the pewter, causing those who could afford to feast on such dinnerware to succumb to lead poisoning after consuming tomato-infused meals.

During the early 1700s, European colonists brought the tomato back to the Americas. In the northern colonies, it was predominantly cultivated for decorative purposes, while in the southern regions, it was grown for its fruit. Its popularity continued to rise.

Only in the early 1900s did tomatoes become widely popular across the United States. (A History of Tomatoes, n.d.)

Presently, tomatoes are cultivated globally and play a prominent role in international culinary creations. They are nurtured in household gardens as well as on industrial farms.

Tomatoes are consumed fresh, cooked in various recipes, and transformed into goods that fill our grocery store aisles. They stand as the most favored domestically cultivated vegetable crop in the nation.

A FRUIT OR A VEGETABLE?

In 1893, a Supreme Court ruling settled the tomato's identity crisis, declaring it a vegetable for tariff purposes despite its botanical fruit status. The debate arose from a tariff act imposing taxes on vegetables, leading vegetable merchants to claim tomatoes as fruits to avoid the tax. The Nix family, facing a tariff from Edward L. Hedden at the port of New York, took the case to court. Despite the botanical truth, the defense argued tomatoes were commonly treated as vegetables in trade and commerce. The Supreme Court unanimously sided with this perspective, emphasizing how tomatoes are eaten – in savory dishes, not as desserts. This quirky legal twist continues to flavor discussions, influencing state designations like New Jersey naming the tomato its state vegetable in 2005. (Eschner, 2017)

The botanical categorization of fruits and vegetables relies mainly on the configuration and role of the plant component in consideration.

Fruits originate from flowers, encompass seeds, and contribute to the plant's reproductive cycle. Examples of familiar fruits include apples, oranges, mangoes, and grapes.

Conversely, vegetables are different parts of plants, such as roots, stems, leaves, or additional supportive plant segments. Recognizable vegetables encompass potatoes, lettuce, carrots, beets, and celery.

In the realm of cooking, the system of categorizing fruits and vegetables undergoes substantial changes compared to their botanical classification.

In the culinary context, fruits and vegetables are employed and utilized primarily based on their taste characteristics.

Broadly, a fruit exhibits a tender consistency and leans towards sweetness, possibly with a hint of tartness or tanginess. It is most fitting for desserts, baked goods, smoothies, preserves, or simply enjoyed as a standalone snack.

In contrast, a vegetable commonly presents a milder and potentially bitter taste. It typically possesses a more robust texture than fruit and while some can be enjoyed raw, cooking may be necessary. Vegetables are well-suited for savory preparations like stir-fries, stews, salads, and casseroles.

thought bubble: *Ever tried convincing a carrot to join the dessert menu?*

Botanically, tomatoes are classified as fruit since they contain seeds and emerge from flowers. However, in the culinary realm, tomatoes are regarded as vegetables due to their common uses in various dishes. (Ld, 2018).

Why Homegrown Tomatoes Are Better

The Environmental Working Group (EWG), a non-profit entity, has published its 2023 Dirty Dozen compilation, pinpointing the fruits and vegetables most tainted with traces of pesticides.

According to research, both producers and consumers could face exposure to pesticides that pose significant toxicity risks to them and the surrounding environment. The study uncovered that 75% of conventionally grown fresh produce available in the United States carries traces of potentially hazardous chemical pesticides. (Dione et al., 2023).

On the other hand, homegrown tomatoes have a number of benefits; let's discuss them one by one.

1. Tomatoes provide an excellent supply of essential vitamins.

Interestingly, one little tomato can offer approximately 40% of the daily recommended minimum of vitamin C. Isn't it fantastic?

But not only that. Tomatoes also deliver vitamin A, promoting immunity, vision, and skin well-being, along with vitamin K, which is beneficial for bone health.

Moreover, tomatoes furnish potassium, a crucial nutrient supporting heart function, muscle contractions, and the upkeep of optimal blood pressure and fluid balance. Who says multitasking affects efficiency?

2. They safeguard cardiovascular well-being.

Tomatoes are pretty considerate. They know how to take care of your heart. That's why they encompass an antioxidant named lycopene (responsible for their red hue). Research indicates that elevated blood levels of lycopene correlate with reduced mortality rates in individuals with metabolic syndrome, a group of risk factors heightening the likelihood of heart disease, diabetes, and stroke.

3. They promote eye health.

Lycopene benefits your eyes, and tomatoes house eye-protective elements like lutein and beta-carotene. These compounds bolster vision and safeguard against eye issues such as cataracts and macular degeneration.

4. They enhance gastrointestinal well-being.

Did you know that 95% of tomatoes are made up of water? Well, now you do!!

They also contain an adequate amount of fiber. This is precisely why they can be beneficial for those susceptible to constipation.

5. They could assist in warding off complications related to diabetes.

Tomatoes could serve as a safeguarding dietary choice for individuals with type 2 diabetes. In a particular study, those with diabetes who added cooked tomatoes to their diet for a month observed a reduction in lipid peroxidation (Rdn, 2023). This process involves free radicals attacking fat, causing damage that elevates the risk of heart disease.

6. They can play a role in promoting skin well-being.

Studies have discovered that the blend of tomato paste and olive oil acts as a defense against sun damage and enhances the synthesis of pro-collagen, a molecule crucial for maintaining skin structure and firmness.

Now, you won't have to spend extra money on skin treatments.

Researchers also posit that the pivotal factor is lycopene found in tomatoes, with its peak concentration in cooked forms, and olive oil facilitates
its absorption from the digestive system into the bloodstream (Rdn, 2023).

7. They might aid in shielding against cancer.

Observational research has established connections between the intake of
the prominent compound in tomatoes, lycopene, and reduced occurrences
of prostate, ovarian, lung, and stomach cancers. (Chicago Health & By
Cynthia Sass, MPH, RD, health.com, 2023).

TOMATO CLASSIFICATIONS

Tomatoes can primarily be classified into two types, namely hybrid and
heirloom tomatoes.

*thought bubble: When it comes to hybrid tomatoes, plant breeders play
the role of matchmakers, orchestrating floral rendezvous for tomatoes like a
high-stakes dating game. It's like the tomato version of "The Bachelor," but
instead of roses, they exchange pollen packets. These tomatoes are basically the
result of a carefully curated plant Tinder, where left-swipes and right-swipes
determine the genetic destiny of the next tomato generation. And just like in
human relationships, sometimes there's a surprise twist, and you end up with
a tomato that's a bit of an oddball – the rebel of the vegetable patch.*

In other words, a hybrid tomato is produced through the deliberate
cross-pollination of two distinct plant varieties by plant breeders. This
results in an offspring, or hybrid, inheriting the most favorable traits from
both parent plants. While cross-pollination naturally transpires among
members of the same plant species, hybridization involves a controlled
pollination process to guarantee that specific plants are crossed, aiming for

the desired blend of attributes like increased size or enhanced resistance to diseases. The development of a hybrid usually demands an extended period, often spanning several years. (Hybrid Tomatoes | Varieties | California Summer Winds, n.d.)

In short, hybrid tomatoes are a product of crossbreeding various varieties, frequently designed to enhance productivity or develop resistance against pests and similar challenges.

On the other hand, heirloom tomatoes originate from preserved seeds passed down for generations. Alternatively, they might have been cultivated in the initial phases of commercial breeding at least half a century ago and subsequently transmitted. Farmers retain seeds from superior tomatoes, employing them for further cultivation. Consequently, heirloom varieties closely resemble their predecessors, with lineage tracing back over 100 years.

Honestly, they are the celebrities of the tomato world, boasting a family tree so extensive that even genealogists would be envious!

Another characteristic that makes them different is that they require fertilization through a method called open-pollination, where pollen is transported by bees, insects, birds, wind, water, or alternative mechanisms to facilitate self- or cross-pollination. This process involves no human interference and guarantees that the seeds will give rise to seedlings retaining the majority of the traits of their parental plant.

However, the fact that a plant results from open pollination doesn't automatically classify it as an heirloom. Put differently, every heirloom arises from open-pollination, but not every open-pollinated plant qualifies as an heirloom. (Fincher, 2021).

On the basis of plants, tomatoes can be divided into two categories, namely determinate and indeterminate tomatoes.

Compact and small in size, determinate tomatoes are plants that reach a specific height, pause their growth, and subsequently flower and produce all their fruit within a brief timeframe. The harvesting window for determinate tomatoes is typically brief, rendering them excellent options for canning.

Indeterminate tomatoes persist in their growth, flowering, and fruit-setting until the initial fall frost halts them. Consequently, the harvesting duration for indeterminate varieties frequently spans 2 or 3 months. While the yields are typically more substantial than those of determinate types, they tend to mature later. Indeterminate tomatoes are expansive and sprawling plants, often thriving when cultivated in wire cages or guided by stakes. (In Regards to Tomatoes, What Is Meant by the Terms Determinate and Indeterminate?, n.d.)

These were the basic classifications of tomatoes. But there is a large number of different varieties of tomatoes found across the globe. We'll discuss some of the most popular varieties in the coming chapters.

THE BASIC NEEDS OF TOMATOES

Tomatoes, like any plant, have fundamental needs crucial for their optimal growth. Adequate sunlight, typically 6-to 8 hours daily, facilitates photosynthesis, promoting robust development. Well-drained, nutrient-rich soil ensures proper root health, essential for nutrient absorption.

It's as if tomatoes have their own version of a wellness retreat – sunbathing sessions for that healthy glow and a spa day for their roots.

Regular watering maintains consistent moisture levels, preventing drought stress and blossom-end rot. Appropriate support, such as stakes or cages, prevents sprawling and enhances air circulation, reducing the risk of diseases.

Failure to meet these needs can impede growth. Insufficient sunlight weakens plants, leading to stunted growth and diminished yields. Poor soil quality results in nutrient deficiencies, affecting overall health.

thought bubble: So, it turns out tomatoes are drama queens in the garden – inconsistent watering makes them wilt faster than a poorly delivered punchline. And don't get them started on neglecting support; it's like skipping leg day at the tomato gym, and suddenly, branches start staging a tomato rebellion. So, folks, remember, keep those tomatoes hydrated and emotionally supported – you wouldn't want your garden turning into a vegetable soap opera!

Here are some of the tips to grow healthy tomatoes. You will learn about all these in detail in the coming chapters.

1. Light

Tomato seedlings require intense, unobstructed light. Unless cultivated in a greenhouse, the optimal choice involves employing artificial plant lighting for 14 to 18 hours daily.

To prevent seedlings from becoming elongated, maintain proximity to fluorescent grow lights, ensuring a distance of only a few inches. Adjust the lights (or lower the plants) with the seedlings' growth. When transitioning them outdoors, opt for the sunniest section in your vegetable garden for planting.

When establishing your garden plot, select a spot that gets a minimum of 6 to 8 hours of direct sunlight. Tomatoes thrive and bear fruit when exposed to ample sunlight.

2. Air

For robust stems, allow tomato plants to sway in the breeze, a natural occurrence outdoors. If initiating seedlings indoors, ensure adequate air circulation to mimic this effect.

Generate airflow by activating a fan over them for five to 10 minutes twice daily. Alternatively, gently agitate tomato plants by softly stroking your hand back and forth across their tops multiple times each day.

3. Soil pH

Ensure your soil offers the appropriate environment for tomatoes before planting. Tomatoes thrive in slightly acidic soil, ideally maintaining a pH ranging from 6.2 to 6.8. Verify the soil pH at home or obtain a soil examination from your nearby extension agency, which will also detect any nutrient insufficiencies.

Incorporate compost into the soil prior to planting tomatoes. Additionally, enhance plantings mid-season by side-dressing with compost to supplement nutrients. An alternative approach involves using a tomato-specific fertilizer every two weeks throughout the growing season, commencing at planting time. Given that tomatoes are nutrient-intensive, maintaining a consistent nutrient supply is crucial.

Believe me or not, compost is the tomato's version of a gourmet meal – a delightful buffet for their underground taste buds. They're gonna be super happy when they get enough of it.

4. Right time

Transplant tomatoes into the open once the risk of frost in your cultivation zone has diminished and soil temperatures reach a minimum of

60°F (16°C). Optimal conditions for outdoor tomato planting include night temperatures surpassing 50°F (10°C). Ensure tomato seedlings raised indoors undergo a hardening-off process to aid their acclimatization before transplantation.

5. Planting depth

Plant your tomato seedlings deeper than their potted depth, burying them up to the uppermost leaves. This method encourages the development of roots along the entire stem, fostering a sturdier plant with increased root mass. Whether creating a deep hole or opting for a shallow trench, laying the plant horizontally allows it to correct and grow towards sunlight naturally. Exercise caution to avoid driving the tomato stake or cage into the buried stem during this process.

6. Water

Ensure tomato plants receive consistent and thorough watering while fruits are maturing. In periods of high temperatures or drought, additional watering may be necessary. If plants appear wilted for a significant part of the day, provide hydration. In the absence of rain, aim for approximately an inch of supplementary water each week. Direct water at the plant's base or utilize a soaker hose to prevent leaf splashing, reducing the risk of disease.

Once the fruit initiates ripening, reduce the watering frequency. Moderating water supply encourages the plant to concentrate sugars, enhancing the flavor of the fruit. However, avoid withholding water to an extent that induces persistent wilting and stress, as this may result in blossom drop and potential fruit loss.

7. Mulch

Delay applying mulch until the soil has had an opportunity to warm up. While mulching preserves water and shields plants from soil-borne diseases, it also provides shade and lowers soil temperature. Once temperatures stabilize at a warmer level, apply a layer of mulch to maintain moisture.

Just remember, mulch is like the garden's cozy sweater – don't put it on too early, or your tomatoes might start planning a tropical vacation, thinking it's perpetually winter!

8. Space

Provide ample space for tomato seedlings to expand by thinning them to one robust plant per cell or small container. Trim less vigorous, smaller seedlings in favor of the strongest grower, ensuring adequate space for tomato plants. Overcrowded conditions impede growth, inducing stress and increasing the risk of later disease. Transfer tomato seedlings to individual 4-inch pots once they develop their initial set of true leaves. Prior to garden planting, ensure proper hardening of seedlings.

9. Support

Provide support to your tomato plants when they reach a height of 10 to 12 inches. Utilize tomato cages, string trellises, durable wooden or metal stakes with ties, or other robust structures to maintain the plants' upright posture. Indeterminate tomato varieties generally require sturdier supports compared to determinate types. Nevertheless, even determinate tomatoes can benefit from stakes or cages to ensure they remain upright as they start bearing fruit.

All these were the basic needs of the tomato plant. From light and air to soil conditions, watering, and proper spacing, each element contributes to a thriving and productive tomato garden. By addressing these essentials, you provide the optimal environment for tomatoes to flourish, ensuring a bountiful harvest.

In the end...

In this chapter, you explored the fascinating history of the humble tomato, unraveling its botanical identity and the lingering fruit versus vegetable debate. Delving into the benefits of cultivating homegrown tomatoes, from health advantages to avoiding pesticides, highlighted their superiority. The classifications of tomatoes, be it heirloom or hybrid, determinate or indeterminate, provided insight into the diverse world of tomato varieties. Additionally, a glimpse into the basic needs of tomatoes set the stage for in-depth discussions to follow. In the next chapter, we'll delve into selecting quality seeds for your home garden.

So, continue reading to enhance your knowledge of tomato-logy.

Chapter Two

Starting Off Right with the Ultimate Tomato Seeds

"Don't judge each day by the harvest you reap but by the seeds that you plant." – Robert Louis Stevenson

It is time to dive into the amazing world of tomato varieties and help you find those top-notch seeds. In this chapter, we'll discuss the most popular kinds of tomatoes, and here's the cool part – we're not just stopping there.

Ever wondered how to store the seeds of your favorite tomato plants? Well, I'm spilling the beans (or seeds) on that too, so you can keep your seed stash thriving.

So, let's get started!

As mentioned before, there is an enormous variety of tomatoes. All tomatoes are the fruits of the *Solanum lycopersicum* plant, even though they are commonly denoted and utilized as vegetables in culinary applications.

The mouth-watering fact about tomatoes is that they possess a crisp, gentle flavor and are generally crimson. However, they are also available in alternative hues such as yellow, orange, and purple.

And for my health-conscious readers, tomatoes are abundant in nutrients like vitamin C and contain antioxidants like beta-carotene and lycopene, providing various health advantages.

So, what are you waiting for? Let's grab the trowel and rush to the garden. But, wait a second!

There's an almost uncountable variety of tomatoes out there. Which one should you grow? In the following sections, you'll learn the four major kinds of tomatoes and their most popular varieties.

You can go through the description of each one of them one by one and decide for yourself which one you like. However, factors like which variety can grow in the region you live in should be considered, too.

Globe Tomatoes

The first major kind of tomatoes are considered the standard-sized tomatoes that you frequently see in stores. Globe tomatoes present a gentle taste that enhances various dishes. While the majority are red, various varieties are in yellow and green hues. These tomatoes seldom split, and the vegetation is renowned for generating abundant harvests on robust vines. They can be perfect for your garden. Let's see what different varieties of globe tomatoes have to offer.

1. Bellini Tomatoes

Bellini tomatoes boast an indeterminate growth pattern, making them a resilient and productive choice for home gardeners. As a hybrid variety, they offer a harmonious blend of characteristics that contribute to their appeal.

With a relatively short 65 days to maturity, these tomatoes swiftly transform from seed to flavorful fruition. Sporting large, orange cocktail-sized fruits, Bellini tomatoes stand out not just in size but in taste. Their exceptional flavor, accompanied by great texture and commendable resistance to cracking, makes them a delightful addition to culinary endeavors.

Furthermore, these tomatoes exhibit solid general disease resistance, adding to their overall reliability in cultivation.

2. Better Boy

Next in the list are Better Boy tomatoes, classified as indeterminate hybrids, which bring a remarkable combination of qualities to the gardening scene. Requiring a moderate 75 days to reach maturity, these tomatoes unfold as a spectacular midseason delight.

The plump and juicy deep red tomatoes steal the spotlight, boasting an extraordinary flavor profile. The fruits exhibit a perfect balance of juiciness and firmness, making them a culinary delight.

What sets Better Boy apart is its high adaptability, thriving seamlessly in almost any climate. With the added advantage of VFNASt resistance, this variety stands out as a robust and flavorful choice for gardeners seeking both reliability and taste in their tomato harvests. It is like hitting two jackpots with a single spin of a wheel of fortune.

You'll see the code on the seed packets or, if you are buying young plants, on the tag next to the variety name.

VFNASt means that the plant is resistant to many insects and plant diseases that are:

- V: Verticillium Wilt

- F: Fusarium Wilt

- N: Nematodes

- T: Tobacco Mosaic Virus

- A: Alternaria Stem Canker

- St: Stemphylium Gray Leaf Spot

3. BHN 589 F1

BHN 589 F1, a determinate hybrid tomato variety that unfolds its wonders in just 75 days to maturity. With resistance against Fusarium wilt races 1 and 2, as well as protection from mosaic virus and Verticillium wilt, these tomatoes boast robust defenses.

The surprise lies in the harmonious blend of fruit quality, extended shelf life, and truly delightful flavor that they offer. The semi-determinate plants exhibit a larger size compared to compact determinate tomatoes, making them a standout choice.

Whether in an open field, hoop house, or greenhouse, BHN 589 F1 proves its excellence, making it a versatile and rewarding addition to any gardening venture.

4. Celebrity Tomatoes

It is a semi-determinate hybrid that takes center stage in just 70 days, offering a swift journey from planting to harvest. Boasting disease resistance and crack resistance, these tomatoes prove to be a reliable choice for various culinary endeavors.

Whether you're making sandwiches, slicing for salads, enjoying snacks, or creating flavorful bruschetta, Celebrity tomatoes rise to the occasion.

The large, prized tomatoes not only fulfill your "basic" tomato needs but also add a burst of flavor to your dishes. With its all-around versatility and dependable performance, Celebrity stands as a go-to option for a range of culinary delights.

5. *Crimson Carmello*

Crimson Carmello is an indeterminate hybrid tomato that embraces a leisurely 75-day journey to maturity. This variety stands resilient against LB, TMV, N, and V, ensuring a robust defense.

Picture this: heavy clusters of round fruit adorning sturdy and uniform plants. What truly sets Crimson Carmello apart is its remarkable combination of generous fruit size and well-developed flavor, a rare feat for an early hybrid tomato.

This tantalizing blend of characteristics makes it a standout choice for those seeking both early yields and a delightful taste experience in their tomato harvest.

6. *Early Girl*

Early Girl, an indeterminate hybrid tomato that takes a swift 57 days to reach maturity. Favored for its resilience against F 1-2 and V, this early-season delight offers meaty, ripe, red fruits weighing in at 4 to 6 ounces.

The firm texture and blemish-resistant skin make it a visually and gastronomically pleasing choice. Early Girl doesn't just stop at quality – it's a prolific producer, delivering heavy yields on robust and hardy vines. For those eager to savor the goodness of tomatoes early in the season, Early

Girl stands out as a reliable and flavorful option in the world of hybrid tomatoes.

7. Fantastic tomatoes

They really are fantastic!

These are indeterminate hybrid tomatoes that unfold their wonders over 80 days. Not just a delight for your taste buds, this variety boasts disease resistance and crack resistance, ensuring robust and visually appealing fruits.

Imagine tasty, globe-shaped, scarlet red fruits ranging from 3 to 5 inches – almost crack-free. The richness of their flavor adds a savory touch to your culinary creations. Fantastic doesn't just stop at taste; its heavy yields make it an excellent choice for canning. With a medium size that strikes the right balance, Fantastic stands out as a fantastic addition to your tomato garden.

8. Legend

It is a determinate open-pollinated tomato variety that swiftly matures in just 68 days. With a robust defense against LB disease, Legend stands out as one of the earliest maturing slicing tomatoes.

They're big, 4 to 5 inch, glossy red fruits with a uniform round shape, making them a visual delight. What makes Legend unique is its parthenocarpic nature, contributing to the consistent and impressive fruit production.

Parthenocarpic fruits are developed without fertilization. As a result they are seedless.

Additionally, Legend showcases cold tolerance, making it a reliable choice even in cooler climates. For those seeking early, vibrant, and cold-resistant slicing tomatoes, Legend emerges as a noteworthy contender in the world of tomato varieties.

9. Mountain Merit

Mountain Merit, a determinate hybrid tomato that takes a patient 75 days to reach maturity. Resilient against F 1-3, LB TSWV, V IR, AB, and N, this variety stands strong with excellent resistance. Mountain Merit boasts medium to large, 8 to 10-ounce deep red fruits.

What makes it truly stand out is its crack resistance, ensuring pristine and visually appealing tomatoes. With its exceptional resistance to Late Blight and other challenges, Mountain Merit emerges as the perfect choice for slicing tomatoes, offering a combination of size, flavor, and resilience for a delightful gardening experience.

10. Oregon Spring

Oregon Spring a determinate open-pollinated tomato variety that matures in a brisk 60 days. With resilience against V, this early bloomer sets an abundance of meaty fruits, weighing in at 3 to 5 ounces, and promises excellent flavor.

The compact plants of Oregon Spring defy cool weather, consistently setting fruits throughout the season. Noteworthy is its nearly seedless nature, enhancing the overall culinary experience. Whether you're dreaming of homemade ketchup or flavorful sauces, Oregon Spring emerges as the perfect choice, offering a compact, resilient, and delicious addition to your tomato garden.

11. Roadster Tomatoes

Roadster is a determinate hybrid tomato that matures in a brisk 70 days. This salad variety not only brings early maturity to the table but also boasts an extra-large size. The attractive red fruits are substantial and smooth-shouldered, contributing to a visually pleasing appearance.

Roadsters are different from others because of its superior flavor, making it a go-to choice for those who prioritize taste in their salad tomatoes. Particularly well-suited for Northern climates with short growing seasons, the Roadster emerges as a great option for those seeking both early harvests and impressive size in their tomato varieties.

12. Siletz

It is a determinate, parthenocarpic tomato variety that matures in a swift 60 days. Resistant to F1 and V, Siletz stands out as one of the most reliable slicing tomatoes for your garden. The flavor-packed red tomatoes not only promise a delightful taste but also come nearly seedless, enhancing the overall culinary experience.

As the season unfolds, you can expect several bursts of ripe tomatoes, adding a continuous supply of freshness to your harvest. Siletz emerges as a dependable choice, delivering both reliability and flavor for those seeking a consistently rewarding slicing tomato in their garden.

13. Super Bush

Super Bush is a determinate container hybrid tomato designed for toughness and disease resistance. Ideal for container gardening, this variety ensures a reliable and bountiful harvest. Despite its compact nature, Super Bush doesn't compromise on quality, producing a prolific crop of juicy and flavorful fruits of medium size.

Whether you're limited on space or simply prefer container gardening, Super Bush stands out as a resilient and fruitful choice, making it a convenient option for those looking to cultivate tomatoes in containers without sacrificing taste and yield.

With this you have learned about the 13 most popular globe tomato varieties. But we've only just kicked off; there's much more in store. So, get ready to tantalize your tomato buds!

BEEFSTEAK TOMATOES

Coming to the type of tomatoes we hear about, all the time. The beefsteak tomatoes are the larger kinds, often weighing in at more than a pound per tomato. The varieties are rich in classic flavor.

The term first appeared in an 1869 seed catalog, describing slices of a specialty tomato as being "as solid and meaty as a beefsteak."

In this list, I've mentioned the 17 most popular beefsteaks, even though there are plenty more. So, let's dive in.

1. Beefsteak

In the world of tomatoes, the Beefsteak variety stands as a true marvel. With an indeterminate growth pattern and an open-pollinated nature, this tomato takes its time, maturing over a span of 80 days. They are large, solid, and brilliantly red fruits, each weighing up to a staggering 2 pounds.

The Beefsteak isn't just about size; it's a sensory delight – juicy, meaty, and bursting with flavor. As you slice into its excellence, you're met with a rich, sub-acid taste that elevates any culinary creation. The Beefsteak is more than a tomato; it's an experience, a testament to the vibrant diversity within the world of tomatoes.

2. Big Beef

Big Beef is an indeterminate hybrid tomato that matures in 73 days. With VFFNTASt resistance, it is a robust choice adaptable to virtually any climate, triumphing over challenging growing conditions. Beyond its resilience, Big Beef brings an old-fashioned, rich flavor to the table, making it a timeless and reliable option for tomato enthusiasts seeking both adaptability and a classic tomato taste in their garden.

3. Brandywine Pink

Dating back to 1885, you'll notice their unique upright growth, producing one to two tomatoes per cluster. Patience pays off in about 85 days, rewarding you with hefty 14-ounce tomatoes. Their rich, slightly sweet, and spicy flavor makes them perfect for fresh bites or cooking adventures – try pan-frying, barbecuing, simmering, or exploring new recipes with them.

4. Chef's Choice Orange Hybrid

It is a hybrid heirloom that not only adds beauty to your garden but also promises easy enjoyment. With a harmonious taste, it brings resistance to diseases and cracking. The indeterminate plant generously yields fruits perfect for slicing, soups, and sauces. It's a delightful addition to both your garden and your kitchen!

5. Cherokee Purple

Cherokee stands out as another excellent heirloom choice. You'll experience a unique journey with this tomato, starting with an initial smokiness and ending with a sweet aftertaste. With its purple or red exterior, it reveals a dark red interior. Each tomato, weighing around 13 ounces, matures in about 85 days.

6. Tamandi Hybrid

What's universally adored about these tomatoes is not just their traditional heirloom taste but also their resilience to diseases and remarkable productivity. These indeterminate plants yield a plethora of fruits, each weighing six ounces and maturing in approximately 72 days.

Emitting a delightful aroma, they boast a rich, balanced flavor blending acidity and sweetness. They can add a unique flavor to your meals. When people reminisce about the classic taste of tomatoes, this is precisely the flavor they reference.

7. Super Steak Hybrid

These colossal tomatoes, boast an average fruit size of approximately two pounds and a maturity timeline of 80 days. You can expect a classic taste from Super Steak Hybrid. They strike a perfect equilibrium between acidity and sweetness, coupled with a substantial, meaty texture.

8. The Brandy Boy Hybrid

A crossbreed of Brandy Wine, this hybrid inherits the delectable Brandy Wine flavor with a well-calibrated blend of acidity and sweetness, tilting slightly towards the sweeter spectrum. Cultivating in a more rounded form with neater growth, it boasts disease resistance and a bountiful harvest. These tomatoes reach an approximate weight of 14 ounces and ripen within around 75 days.

9. Delicious

The moniker says it all – Delicious beefsteak tomatoes burst with flavor, yielding sizable fruits ranging from one to two pounds. Embracing that classic taste we often mention, characterized by a perfect blend of acidity and sweetness, this variety excels as a superb slicing tomato, reaching maturity in around 77 days.

10. Orange Slice Hybrid

With an average weight of approximately one pound per tomato, get ready for a vibrant burst of color in your tomato patch. Growing consistently and boasting a texture that's both firm and juicy, these tomatoes are ready for harvest in around 75 days. Offering a full-bodied flavor, they strike a rich equilibrium between acidity and sweetness.

11. Damsel Hybrid

It's a hybrid that delivers exceptional heirloom flavor, showcasing uniform fruits averaging around 12 ounces. Although an indeterminate tomato, it's promoted as petite, reaching a modest height of approximately six feet. You can expect a timeline of approximately 70 days from seed to harvest.

12. Pink Pounder Hybrid

You'll appreciate the Pink Pounder hybrid in your tomato garden. Picture each tomato, balancing heft and juiciness at one pound. In 75 days, your patience pays off with a bountiful harvest. You can enjoy the creamy texture and sweet pink hues of these tomatoes, offering a flavor profile that gracefully balances acidity and sweetness.

13. Big Pink Hybrid

You'll find Big Pink Hybrid a mid-sized beefsteak tomato with a harmonious blend of sweetness and acidity, leaning slightly towards the sweet side. Sporting an attractive rosy outer layer, these tomatoes weigh in at an average of eight to 10 ounces and reach harvest readiness in approximately 75 days.

14. The Sunny Boy Hybrid

These yellow tomatoes are impossible to overlook, standing out in your garden. Averaging around a pound each, they're ideal sliced on a sandwich, featuring a tender texture and a harmonious sweet and acidic flavor. Maturing in about 75 days, this variety yields abundantly.

15. Super Beefsteak

Another sizable variant, this plant yields fruits averaging around 17 ounces and matures in 80 days. You will experience an equilibrium of acidity and sweetness coupled with a substantial interior. This variety generates numerous fruits per plant.

16. Dark Star Hybrid

If you fancy the delightful blend of savory sweetness, the Dark Star Hybrid is your go-to. These plants yield abundant fruits, each weighing around eight ounces. They can make your dishes even better because of their profound tomato taste without the sharp acidity. They reach maturity in approximately 75 to 80 days and exhibit notable resistance to blight.

17. Orange Wellington Hybrid

These vivid, medium to large beefsteak tomatoes are almost devoid of seeds. They have a sweet, low-acid taste and excel not only as fantastic slicers but also when roasted. Resilient to various diseases, this robust beefsteak tomato plant yields consistently throughout the season. The fruits weigh approximately 20 ounces each, ensuring an abundant supply for all.

Isn't it awesome?

Having a diverse range of flavorful and vibrant tomatoes in your garden and in your kitchen. But that's still not it. There are more awesome varieties of this fruit cum vegetable. I believe, as a tomato enthusiast you have the right to know about them!

So, let's continue.

PASTE TOMATOES

If you're someone who cannot imagine their life without delicious sauces, this section is especially for you. Paste tomatoes are generally sought out to make sauces and home canning for long-term preservation. Let's learn about them.

1. Amish Paste

Renowned for canning, the Amish Paste tomatoes stand out as one of the most sizable paste varieties. Yielding oxheart-shaped, meaty tomatoes that can reach up to 12 ounces, these tomatoes are a mainstay on our suburban homestead.

These are indeterminate; red tomatoes mature in 85 days, late in the season.

2. Roma VF

A homestead essential, the Roma VF paste tomato yields bright red, plum-shaped fruits, averaging around 2 oz—ideal for paste, sauces, or puree. Initially introduced in 1963 by the Joseph Harris Seed Company in Rochester, New York, this widely adapted variety boasts resistance to fusarium wilt and verticillium.

These are semi-determinate red tomatoes that mature in 75 days, early in the season.

3. Principe Borghese

The quintessential Italian sun-dried tomato, Principe Borghese, features clusters of 1 oz plum tomatoes traditionally sun-dried for winter or crafted into a flavorful sauce. Plants can be brought indoors to ripen remaining fruit, often hung in a shed or garage. Alternatively, clusters hung indoors typically stay preserved for about a week.

These are also semi-determinate red tomatoes that mature in 70 days early in the season.

4. San Marzano

A highly favored choice among homesteaders, San Marzano, derives its name from its Italian place of origin. The condensed plants yield abundant 2 to 3 inch meaty and flavorful fruits. With crack-resistant attributes, these plants are particularly suitable for novice gardeners.

These are Semi-determinate red tomatoes that reach maturity in 85 days during the midseason.

5. Speckled Roman

The Striped Roman tomato, also known as Speckled Roman, is a prolific plant producing meaty, 4 to 6-inch fruits with red hue and yellow stripes along their length.

These are the indeterminate red-yellow bi-colored tomatoes that mature in 75 days during the midseason.

6. Gilbertie Tomato

Gilbertie, an heirloom paste tomato, yields 7-inch elongated fruits resembling chili peppers, weighing approximately 10 to 12 oz, with a meaty, flavorful profile and minimal seeds—ideal for canning as whole tomatoes, sauce, or salsa.

These are indeterminate tomatoes with red and green shoulders that mature in 85 days during the midseason.

7. Howard German

A pre-1900s heritage variety, this heirloom yields red fruits ranging from 3 to 9 oz, showcasing considerable variability in shapes, resembling frying peppers to plum shapes. The fruits have a dry, meaty flesh, making them flavorful and ideal for sauce.

These are indeterminate red tomatoes that reach maturity in 90 days during the mid-late season.

8. Italian Heirloom

For those seeking substantial, meaty fruits with minimal seeds, the Italian Heirloom fits the bill! These plants yield copious quantities of massive 12 to 20-oz red fruits and exhibit resilience to various diseases, including Late Blight—a must-have for your homestead garden.

Italian Heirloom tomatoes are indeterminate red tomatoes that reach maturity in 80 days during the mid-late season.

9. Ten Fingers of Naples

An excellent determinate cultivar, this variety yields abundant clusters of fruits in long trusses, with 5 to 6 inch fruits weighing approximately 3 oz each. The flavor is delightful, being sweet and rich, making it ideal for crafting some of the most flavorful sauces. Additionally, these plants exhibit resistance to diseases.

These determinate red tomatoes reach maturity in 75 days during the midseason.

10. HEINZ 1350 VF

Perfect for sauce and suitable for gardens with shorter seasons, the Heinz 1350 VF tomato yields medium-sized, round fruits and boasts resistance to Curly Top Virus.

These are the determinate red tomatoes that mature in 75 days during the midseason.

11. Gezahnte

Gezahnte tomatoes may be rare, but sourcing them online or through seed swaps is rewarding, especially for their resilience in hot, dry climates. Hailing from Italy, these heirlooms yield red, ribbed fruits of about 8 oz throughout the season. Notably, the semi-hollow nature of the fruits makes them excellent for stuffing!

These are the indeterminate red tomatoes that reach maturity in 80 days during the midseason.

12. Costoluto Genovese

An Italian heritage variety renowned for its exceptional flavor, perfect for crafting sauce! These plants yield substantial quantities of uniquely shaped tomatoes with prominent lobes. The flesh is arid, and the seed cavities are petite, making it advisable to collect seeds during the canning preparation process.

These indeterminate red tomatoes mature in 80 days during the midseason.

13. Federle

Federle tomato plants exhibit productivity, yielding moderately large, slender, elongated tomatoes. With their dry flesh and minimal seeds, these heirloom tomatoes are an ideal choice for sauce-making and canning.

Federle are indeterminate tomatoes that are red in color and reach maturity in 90 days during the midseason.

14. Goldman's Italian-American

In search of a sweet, delectable sauce? Goldman's Italian-American tomato is an excellent sauce-making option! These plants yield bell-shaped tomatoes, each weighing about 12 oz. With prolific production, this choice is perfect for homestead gardens.

These indeterminate red tomatoes mature in 80 days during the midseason.

15. Jersey Devil

Jersey Devil tomatoes may have a slow fruit-setting pace, but these plants yield copious harvests. The substantial fruits, reaching lengths of up to 6 inches, boast a sweet and flavorful profile.

These indeterminate red tomatoes reach maturity in 85 days during the midseason.

CHERRY TOMATOES

Cherry tomatoes are more petite and ideal for beginners because they are easier to grow. Not only are these varieties smaller, but they all also grow in clusters. So, without further ado, let's learn about them!

1. Baby Boomer

It produces a substantial, abundant yield, delivering fruit until frost intervenes. Each plant produces 300 vibrant red, one-inch tomatoes throughout the season. As a prolific hybrid, the fruit boasts a complete, sweet taste, perfect for fresh snacking or grilling. 'Baby Boomer' matures fruit within 50 to 55 days on 20 to 25-inch plants, their branches laden heavily, suggesting the use of a cage or alternative support.

2. Maglia Rosa

Tomatoes don't come any more aesthetically pleasing than 'Maglia Rosa.' Featuring ovate fruits measuring 2 to 3 inches, adorned in variegated hues of pink and orange, they dangle like substantial clusters of precious gems.

These flavorful treasures thrive in containers or cascade from a suspended basket. Harvest when they transition to a pink hue for an alluring taste—subtly acidic, sumptuously rich, and sweet. The semi-determinate, open-pollinated plants reach heights of 24 to 36 inches, with tomatoes maturing in 70 days.

3. Sweetheart of the Patio

A semi-determinate hybrid, 'Sweetheart of the Patio,' excels in yield, generating clusters of exceptionally sweet, vibrant red one-inch fruits.

Compact yet robust, copious fruit clusters mature in 68 days on plants ranging from 24 to 36 inches in height. Resilient against late blight, these aesthetically pleasing plants thrive in containers, hanging baskets, or directly in the garden.

4. Tiny Tim

A swiftly maturing heirloom variety, 'Tiny Tim,' yields a profusion of deep red, four-ounce fruits. The fruit ripens within a short 55 to 60 days. Petite plants reach a mature height of 12 to 16 inches and a width of only six inches. Perfect for cultivating in containers on the patio or in hanging baskets, 'Tiny Tim' accommodates some shade. Initially introduced by the University of New Hampshire in 1945.

5. Black Cherry

As an heirloom selection, 'Black Cherry' offers an intricate, sweet taste and sturdy consistency in bite-sized delights. The one-inch fruits mature into a deep mahogany brown, consistently produced by plants throughout the warm summer period. With a growth height of around 60 inches, these plants reach maturity in 64 days. These delightful and exotic nuggets are perfect for snacking and imparting a robust taste to bruschetta, pizzas, and salsas. Naturally resistant to diseases, seeds can be gathered for propagation.

6. Black Pearl

'Black Pearl' showcases a beautifully intense, deep mahogany hue, and its heirloom lineage as a hybrid fusion of 'Black Cherry' imparts a pleasing, intricate taste—sweet with a rich, tangy edge. The robust vines bear abundant clusters of one-and-a-half-inch tomatoes, continuing production until autumn. Growing to a height of 60 inches, these plants necessitate cages or stakes for support. The fruits are delectable for snacking or enhance the allure of bruschetta and pizza, maturing in 65 days.

7. Green Envy

Offering a sweet, juicy choice with a subtle taste, the elongated, one-inch fruits of hybrid 'Green Envy' reach a deep, see-through emerald green upon ripening. These plants maintain continuous production until fall. The robust and substantial tomatoes are perfect for grilling or roasting, contributing a crisp, refreshing flavor to salads and salsas. They mature in 60 to 70 days on plants reaching heights of 63 to 67 inches; support in the form of a cage or stakes is essential.

8. Italian Ice

Exhibiting a sugary sweetness and a gentle, low-acid flavor, 'Italian Ice' is a bountiful hybrid, producing ample clusters of one-inch fruits in a gentle, creamy yellow shade. Abundant clusters emerge throughout summer until frost terminates the plants. Enjoyably chilled for a refreshing salad or snack, these fruits complement pasta or can be transformed into a mild green relish. Plants reach heights of 60 to 72 inches, and the fruits can be harvested within a brisk 65 days.

9. Midnight Snack

'Midnight Snack,' a luscious and attractive variety, stands out as one of the most flavorful purple tomatoes. When cultivated in full sunlight, the fruit showcases striking purple-black shoulders coupled with an olive-purple underside. This intense coloring is attributed to the anthocyanin pigments—healthful antioxidants that render it a delectable, guilt-free snack. These prolific hybrid plants yield one-and-a-half-inch fruits, boasting a well-defined, harmonious taste and a robust texture suitable for salads and grilling. The vines achieve a height of 72 to 84 inches, and the fruits are ready for harvest within a span of 65 to 70 days.

10. Mirabella Blanche

The attractive one-inch spheres of 'Mirabelle Blanche' mature to a see-through pale yellow with a touch of blush pink, forming in extensive clusters. These fruits possess a distinctive, sweet taste complemented by a pleasant acidic tang, rendering them perfect for dehydrating, salads, or grilling. As an open-pollinated heirloom, the seeds are viable for storage and subsequent propagation. Plants obtain a stature of 40 to 48 inches and reach maturity within 75 to 80 days.

11. Orange Sunsugar

Among the sweetest cherry varieties, the one-inch orange fruits of 'Orange Sunsugar' radiate like miniature setting suns on robust and vigorous vines. Packed with nutritional value and boasting a high vitamin A content, the fruits feature thin skin yet excellent crack resistance. Furthermore, they exhibit resistance to fusarium wilt and tobacco mosaic virus. The sturdy hybrid vines are expansive, reaching heights of 84 to 108 inches, necessitating caging for support. These delectable fruits achieve maturity in a mere 62 days.

12. Power Pops

Delicious and tasty, 'Power Pops' yields vibrant crimson one-inch fruits that mature a fortnight ahead of other varieties of cherries.

From Burpee's Boost Compilation of vegetables, these plants are specifically engineered for elevated levels of antioxidants – boasting 40 percent additional carotenoids and 55 percent more lycopene compared to the standard commercial tomato.

This blended variety reaches a modest height of 9 to 12 inches yet exhibits a complete, draping demeanor, rendering it ideal for patio containers and suspended baskets.

The fruits mature swiftly in merely 45 days, rendering it a suitable selection for gardeners experiencing brief summer cultivation periods.

13. Sunchocola

'Sunchocola' is a crossbreed that yields succulent one-inch fruits in a stunning, deep brick-red hue, featuring a rich flavor that combines smokiness and sweetness.

An efficient plant, it forms substantial clusters of fruit throughout the entire summer.

Delicious when plucked directly from the vine or cooked on the barbecue, they also serve as a suitable option for sun-drying or dehydration.

The fruits mature in 67 days on plants reaching a height of 70 inches, displaying resistance to mosaic virus. Support from cages or trellises is essential.

14. Sungold

Among the most favored cherries, the hybrid 'Sungold' boasts tangerine-orange fruits with solid flesh, developing in lengthy, substantial bunches on exceptionally prolific vines that continue to produce until autumn.

The one-inch spheres feature a delightful, sweetly tropical flavor.

Delectable when plucked directly from the vine, grilled, or added to salads, the fruits reach maturity in 57 days.

Plants reach heights of 48 to 60 inches and exhibit resistance to fusarium wilt, nematodes, tobacco mosaic virus, and verticillium wilt. Support through caging or staking is necessary.

15. Supersweet 100

Delicious and full of flavor throughout an extended season, 'Supersweet 100' produces lengthy, substantial clusters of vibrant red one-inch fruits continuously from summer to fall.

A sugary favorite for grilling, salsa, salads, and snacks, this prolific plant can reach heights of 90 to 144 inches and necessitates robust caging – the vines will ascend and traverse the top, descending on the opposite side.

This hybrid exhibits resistance to fusarium wilt, nematodes, and verticillium wilt. The fruits reach maturity in 65 days and are ideal for drying, snacking, salads, and juice.

Having journeyed through the diverse realms of globe, beefsteak, paste, and cherry tomatoes, the next step is to cultivate these delectable varieties in your own garden. Wondering where to find the seeds for these tomato treasures? Let's delve into the exciting world of seed sourcing and embark on your gardening adventure.

With this you have learned about the most popular paste tomatoes. Next in the list are the cutest tomato varieties. You would definitely not want to miss them. So, let's explore the playful charm of cherry tomatoes. Bursting with sweetness and a pop of color, these bite-sized delights are a garden favorite. Whether enjoyed fresh, in salads, or as vibrant snacks, cherry tomatoes bring joy to every harvest.

WHERE TO SOURCE TOMATO SEEDS

The first place will be to try your local nursery, as they might be able to give you more specific seed information. Another good reason for buying seeds locally is that you will be growing the same seeds in the same climate as the nursery. That being said, there are also ample online stores that sell quality seeds at great prices. Aside from different varieties, you will also be able to choose disease-resistant hybrids and organic seeds.

Some of the websites you can visit to buy seeds online are mentioned below.

1. Rare Seeds

If you're not familiar with Baker Creek Heirloom Seeds, it's worth exploring. They exclusively offer heirloom selections, numerous of which come with a fascinating history.

Their assortment of tomato seeds is remarkable, featuring an extensive range of over 100 options. They provide striped cherry tomatoes, beefsteaks, globes, and a diverse array in between.

www.rareseeds.com

2. Botanical Interests

It's another reliable website with a diverse range of tomato varieties and they keep adding more varieties. The seed packets have useful information about the variety written on them.

www.botanicalinterests.com

3. Totally tomatoes

Totally Tomatoes offers an exceptionally vast array of both heirloom and hybrid tomato seeds. Additionally, they retail tomato seedlings (plants), allowing you to bypass the germination process if you prefer.

www.totallytomato.com

4. Seed Savers

Seed Savers is dedicated to safeguarding and disseminating heirloom seed varieties. Numerous cultivars in their collection boast histories spanning decades or even centuries.

For those seeking the most flavorful tomatoes to cultivate, explore Seed Savers' extensive assortment of seeds. They present heirlooms from numerous countries, providing an immense range of tastes, sizes, hues, and growth characteristics.

https://seedsavers.org

5. Fruition Seeds

Fruition Seeds offers an excellent array of tomato seeds. While their collection isn't vast, the diversity is astonishing.

You can discover striped cherry, purple variations, large and small tomatoes, hybrids, and heirlooms. The detailed descriptions for each variety, along with buyer reviews, are incredibly informative.

www.fruitionseeds.com

6. Tomato Fest

The self-proclaimed "tomato enthusiast's haven" is, indeed, the residence of numerous tomato seed options available for purchase. If you're seeking an incredibly extensive assortment, this serves as an excellent starting point.

A particular focus is on compact varieties, perfect for cultivating in limited garden spaces. Notably, the Tasty Wine tomato, standing at a mere 3 feet tall, produces substantial pink beefsteak fruits.

https://www.tomatofest.com/

They also stock scarce and distinctive cultivars, which are discontinued after a specified period. If you enjoy cultivating more experimental tomatoes, this might be precisely what you're searching for.

7. High Mowing Seeds

High Mowing Seed is an excellent choice for those considering farm initiation. They boast an extensive assortment of vegetables, flowers, herbs – you name it.

The tomato variety they offer is substantial, encompassing F1 hybrids, timeless heirlooms, and beyond.

www.highmowingseeds.com

8. Forgotten Heirlooms

Forgotten Heirlooms is a petite online establishment, akin to a family-run business. Nonetheless, the assortment is far from diminutive!

Ranging from micro-dwarf tomatoes to cherry and grape varieties, and extending to substantial slicers, they offer a comprehensive selection. Back a small enterprise while cultivating exceptional tomato (and pepper) plants simultaneously!

www.forgottenheirlooms.com

How to Store Tomato Seeds

Saving your own tomato seeds from one season to the next is straightforward, reducing your seed expenses and eventually allowing you to develop plants tailored to your specific growing environment.

The majority of tomatoes contain 100 seeds or more, meaning you only require a few fruits for seed preservation. It's important to note that seeds from F1 hybrid types won't replicate the original variety, so focus on saving seeds from traditional, open-pollinated tomatoes, often referred to as heirloom or heritage varieties. Let me walk you through the process of storing your seeds step by step.

Step 1: Collecting Tomato Seeds

Gather your seeds from completely matured fruits. Slice the tomato apart, then extract the pulpy content housing the seeds into a glass container. For smaller tomatoes, simply burst them and press out the contents. Add a bit of water to the jar and clearly mark it with the tomato variety.

Step 2: Removing the Gel

The gel enveloping the seeds hinders germination and needs extraction. Allow it to sit for two to five days to initiate fermentation. This process will dismantle the seed coat while eliminating numerous detrimental bacteria and fungi present on the seeds.

Step 3: Cleaning Tomato Seeds

Inspect and softly agitate the jar daily. Once the pulp rises to the surface, indicating the seeds are prepared for cleaning, you might notice a layer of scum. Simultaneously, a majority of the seeds should have settled at the bottom. Gently remove the pulp, then pour the liquid and seeds into a sieve. Rinse the seeds under flowing water, utilizing the rear of a wooden spoon to delicately eliminate any residual material clinging to them.

Step 4: Drying Tomato Seeds

Disperse the seeds on a paper towel to eliminate the majority of moisture, then move them to a surface that's not prone to sticking, like a dinner plate. Let the seeds dry in a warm location away from direct sunlight. The complete drying process usually spans two to three weeks.

Step 5: Storing Tomato Seeds

Carefully transfer the seeds into labeled paper envelopes. Keep them in a dry area at a cool, consistent temperature. Consider placing the envelopes in a tin or another airtight container, along with silica gel crystals to maintain dry air. Seeds have the potential to remain viable for up to five years.

Preserving your own tomato seeds is a straightforward task that brings a sense of profound satisfaction throughout the entire procedure.

PERCY SARGEANT

MOST POPULAR TOMATO VARIETIES

VARIETY	SHAPE	SIZE	TASTE	COLOUR	CLASS	DAYS TO MATURITY
Beefsteak	Round	Large	Rich	Red	Heirloom	80-100
Roma	Plum	Medium	Tangy	Red	Paste	75-85
Cherry	Round	Small	Sweet	Various	Indeterminate	55-75
Brandywine	Beefsteak	Large	Complex	Pink	Heirloom	80-100
San Marzano	Plum	Medium	Intense	Red	Paste	80-90
Celebrity	Round	Medium	Balanced	Red	Hybrid	70
Sungold	Round	Small	Sweet	Orange	Indeterminate	65
Green Zebra	Round	Medium	Tangy	Green	Heirloom	75-80
Early Girl	Round	Medium	Mild	Red	Hybrid	50-62
Black Krim	Beefsteak	Large	Smokey	Purple	Heirloom	70-80
Yellow Pear	Pear	Small	Mild	Yellow	Indeterminate	70
Sweet 100	Round	Small	Sweet	Red	Indeterminate	65
Mortgage Lifter	Beefsteak	Large	Sweet	Pink	Heirloom	80-85
Husky Cherry	Round	Small	Sweet	Red	Hybrid	70
Amish Paste	Plum	Medium	Rich	Red	Paste	80-85

With this, you've learned about different types of tomatoes – globes, beef-steaks, paste, and cherries. We have covered how to grow them, store them, and where to get their seeds.

In the coming chapter, you'll explore the secrets to successful tomato cultivation. We'll dive into the art of planting tomato seeds with optimal germination rates, uncover the best timing for both indoor and outdoor growth. I will also provide you with valuable advice on selecting the right soil and creating ideal conditions to boost germination. So, get ready to cultivate thriving tomato plants with confidence!

Chapter Three

Eagerly Awaiting Those Tomato Sprouts

Imagine this: you listened to a podcast of an expert gardener and their beautiful tomato garden inspired you so much that you are all excited to dive into the world of growing tomatoes. You've got dreams of a tomato jungle in your backyard, but reality hits hard and out of 20 seeds you plant only 2 seeds decide to join the sprouting party. Not exactly the tomato fiesta you envisioned, right?

Well, don't worry! In this chapter, we're about to sprinkle some magic on your tomato-growing journey. We'll reveal the secrets of the best times to plant those seeds, whether you're an indoor or outdoor enthusiast. Plus, we've got the lowdown on the soil secrets and other must-know conditions that might be beneficial in skyrocketing your germination rates.

So, without any further ado, let's get started.

INDOOR OR OUTDOOR GROWING

Quite obviously, tomatoes flourish in outdoor settings if you take care of some specific prerequisites.

So, what do you think these conditions are?

Put simply, your delicate plants need a temperate, sunlit, and shielded location for optimal development. Planting outdoors also known as open-air cultivation needs well-drained, fertile soil enriched with garden compost.

For this purpose, you might need to select a temperate, sun-drenched spot. It is vital and ensures the plants receive abundant sunlight for successful maturation. Besides, planting tomatoes deeply, positioning the initial set of leaves just above the soil surface, and preserving a spacing of 45 to 60cm between plants facilitate their growth.

That's not all!

There are a number of challenges your tiny plants are likely to come across. So, you might need to look after your plants more often. Regular care, encompassing safeguarding against frost, irrigation, and nourishment, contributes to robust plant evolution.

Did you know that outdoor tomatoes thrive in a balmy, sheltered environment, while those cultivated in a greenhouse typically yield an earlier and more abundant crop? Adhering to these criteria results in a plentiful harvest of domestically cultivated tomatoes, presenting a varied array of dimensions, tastes, and consistencies.

You might be wondering why growing tomatoes indoors is different from growing tomatoes outdoors?

Let's discover!

In order to grow tomatoes indoors successfully, you might be required to give attention to imitate their outdoor growing conditions. It is important to know that tomatoes usually thrive in warm climates with long growing seasons, taking about three months for outdoor seeds to become fruit-bearing plants. So, to ensure good indoor growth, it's crucial to copy these conditions.

But what are these conditions?

Your indoor tomato plants need a warm and bright environment, and extra grow lights may be necessary, especially during winter when natural sunlight decreases. It's because a tomato plant requires at least 6 hours of sunlight.

Another important thing to take care of while you grow tomatoes indoors is proper ventilation. Sufficient air circulation is crucial to prevent fungal problems, and shielding from strong drafts is recommended.

As mentioned, tomatoes need full sun, which equals six to eight hours of direct sunlight daily. If there's no sunny window in the area you have decided to grow your tomatoes, you can install grow lights about 1 to 2 inches above the seedlings. It can provide the needed light.

Next condition is availability of appropriate soil. Maintaining the right soil quality is vital for indoor tomato growing. Tomatoes flourish in organically rich, well-draining soil with a slightly acidic to neutral pH.

If all this made you think tomatoes are too choosy, wishing everything to turn out exactly how they want, you are probably right. Because, they might not show up at all if you don't make the arrangements they require.

You might not want to upset them.

So, choose a high-quality, all-purpose organic potting mix for container plantings. You'll learn more about preparing soil for planting tomatoes later in this chapter.

Moving on to the next condition, tomatoes like plenty of water, but at the same time, they need well-drained soil. It's essential to avoid water logging. It sounds a little tricky, and most beginners can't get it right. But you need not worry because we'll discuss how to avoid this common mistake in the coming chapters. For now, you should know that keeping the soil lightly moist, not soggy, can prevent problems like fruit splitting and blossom end rot.

Indoors, room temperatures of 70 to 80 degrees Fahrenheit are suitable, and humidity is generally not a problem.

Just like outdoor tomatoes, fertilizing indoor tomatoes is crucial, and using an organic slow-release fertilizer according to label instructions is recommended. Tomatoes are self-pollinating, but hand pollination or using an oscillating fan to mimic wind conditions may be necessary indoors.

You should also consider the fact that not all tomato varieties can do good when grown indoors. Therefore, choosing suitable tomato varieties for indoor growth is crucial. Compact patio varieties are preferable, with determinate types being a more manageable size.

Pruning, while not necessary, can improve Mortgage Lifter fruitfulness, especially for indeterminate varieties. Planting tomatoes in containers with a minimum diameter of 1 foot is essential. When you repot, avoid disturbing the roots, and choose a container that accommodates the plant's mature size.

Most importantly, indoor tomatoes are vulnerable to various pests and diseases, like aphids and fungal infections. So, what you can do to avoid an unfortunate situation is regularly inspect and clean the plants. Some people prefer moving tomatoes outdoors for the summer. If you are one of them, ensure warm and stable weather conditions, gradually getting the plants used to prevent shock.

To bring tomatoes back inside, you can move them before nighttime temperatures fall below 50 degrees Fahrenheit. Pruning may also be necessary before indoor relocation, and some growers prefer taking cuttings for propagation.

That's it. Easy Peasy, tomato squeezy!

Alright. It might sound complicated but trying all these practically can be an amazing experience and you're probably gonna love it once you start growing your tomatoes.

If you carefully copy these conditions, you'll get a plentiful harvest from your indoor tomatoes, providing fresh and tasty tomatoes throughout the year.

Finding the Ideal Soil Temperature for Seeds

Understanding the optimal timing for planting tomatoes is essential for a fruitful harvest. For this purpose, find the average final frost date in your locality. This information can enable effective planning for your seed initiation project. Most seed packets suggest commencing tomato seeds four to six weeks before the last frost date, ensuring that the seedlings are prepared for transplantation a couple of weeks after this date.

And here's the pro tip!

Starting the process four weeks before the last frost adds a safety margin for unforeseen late frosts. For this, count back four weeks from the last frost date to kickstart the tomato seed initiation process. Vigilantly monitoring and adjusting the routine according to the distinctive requirements of your region can contribute to a successful cultivation venture.

If we talk about soil temperature, your tomatoes need an environment conducive to growth. Optimal soil temperatures of 60°F or higher are vital for their development. This aspect becomes particularly significant when determining the transplanting time.

Before transplanting, you should check the soil temperature with a soil thermometer. This will help you see the distinction from ambient air temperature. This approach can ensure that the soil provides the requisite warmth for the thriving of tomatoes.

The process of planting tomatoes entails precise steps to ensure the production of robust seedlings. From preparing seed trays with loose soil to sowing two to three seeds per cell and covering them with a quarter-inch of starting mix, each phase requires attention to detail. Gently compacting the soil, moistening it with a spray bottle, and maintaining an appropriate germination station contribute to the successful initiation of tomato seeds.

Subsequent stages, including the daily care of seedlings, potential thinning, and the eventual repotting and hardening off, demand consistent attention as well. Your focus on watering, your plants exposure to light, and proper ventilation during these phases is pivotal for the robust development of tomato plants. The hardening-off process, gradually acclimating plants to outdoor conditions, ensures their resilience and adaptability.

In short, the progression from planting tomato seeds to transferring them into the garden requires precise timing, consideration of soil temperature, and diligent care at each step.

A slight mistake at your end can cause great inconvenience for you.

Doing everything carefully will significantly enhance the likelihood of a plentiful harvest of homegrown tomatoes, offering a rewarding outcome for you in the form of fresh and delectable produce.

STARTING TOMATO SEEDS

The wait is finally over. You can now step into your garden. It's time to start tomato seeds.

Embarking on the great adventure of initiating tomato seeds demands a careful approach, encompassing distinct phases ranging from cherry-picking the appropriate tomato variety to relocating the seedlings outdoors. So, let's get started.

Step 1: Selecting the Tomato Seeds

Start the procedure by opting for preferred tomato seeds. You have read about different varieties of tomatoes in the previous chapters and are familiar with the things to consider before picking the seeds.

Some of the factors to consider include choosing certified organic seeds for enthusiasts of organic produce and opting for robust tomato varieties in areas prone to specific plant diseases.

Step 2: Preparing Containers for Planting

Moisten the potting mix before situating it in containers for enhanced effectiveness. Infusing water and permeating it through the soil until it remains compressed yet not dripping wet. Following it, load the containers with the potting soil. You can then delicately compact the soil, leaving it approximately an inch from the brim.

Step 3: Sowing the Tomato Seeds

Construct a 1/4-inch furrow in the potting mix, disperse two to three seeds into the furrow, and cloak them with a light covering of potting mix. Gently compress the mix to ensure optimal seed contact with the soil. If possible, house the containers in a warm setting, and vigilantly observe them daily for soil moisture and germination. Normally, tomato seed germination transpires within a span of 5 to 10 days.

Step 4: Nurturing the Tomato Seedlings

Sustain a warm and humid environment for the seedlings, supplying ample light, preferably via grow lights. Rotate the plants if they incline in a particular direction and introduce a fan or gently sweep your hand through the plants to mimic wind, fostering robust stem development. Once genuine leaves manifest, you can proceed to feeding the seedlings with a diluted liquid fertilizer on a weekly basis.

Step 5: Potting the Tomato Seedlings

Once your seedlings reach a height of 2 to 3 inches with a couple of sets of true leaves, it's time to transfer them to a more capacious container. Load new pots with moist potting mix, and in cases where multiple seeds germinate in the same container, thin the seedlings by gently disentangling interconnected roots or excising surplus seedlings at soil level. Remember to plant each tomato seedling in its new pot marginally deeper than its initial container.

Step 6: Transplanting the Seedlings Outdoors

For the ultimate transition to the garden, opt for a cool or overcast day. Planting the tomatoes deeper than their pot depth fosters new root development along the submerged stem. If indoor plants exhibit excessive height, an alternative is to plant them horizontally in a furrow. Considering the criticality of timing for outdoor transplantation, wait until nighttime temperatures consistently remain above 50 degrees Fahrenheit.

To sum up, the process of initiating tomato seeds is a meticulously orchestrated sequence, encompassing seed selection, container preparation, sowing, seedling care, potting, and eventual outdoor transplantation. Adhering to this exhaustive guide substantially augments the probability of a fruitful harvest, enabling gardeners to relish the fruits of their labor with homegrown, delectable tomatoes.

TRANSPLANTING SEEDLINGS

If you want to enhance the development and yield of your tomato plants, the procedure of repotting tomato seedlings can be a pivotal function, distinguishing between an average plant and one that prospers abundantly.

This essential step involves transferring seedlings into more capacious pots before introducing them to the garden, employing a straightforward yet efficacious method for sturdy growth.

ADVANTAGES OF REPOTTING:

Honestly, repotting tomato seedlings is more of a need than a choice. Let's understand why it's important to replant tomato seedlings.

As a beginner, I saw repotting tomato seedlings as an extra chore, but I later found out how important it can be for the distinct capability of your tomato seedlings to cultivate roots along their stems.

Unlike numerous other plants, tomatoes benefit from being deeply buried, prompting the generation of adventitious roots along their stems. These roots enhance the vitality of the plant, and in regions with high humidity, they might even emerge above ground from stem bumps, contributing to a more extensive and healthier root system.

So, by transplanting seedlings into more spacious pots, you allow their adventitious roots to be invigorated, fostering heightened nutrient absorption and anchoring capabilities.

WHEN TO REPOT:

The right time to repot tomato seedlings is when they attain a height of at least 3 inches and manifest their first true leaves, which emerge subsequent to the initial cotyledons. The first leaves, or cotyledons, are the structures that provide initial nourishment. Repotting is particularly advantageous for leggy seedlings, averting additional elongation and encouraging robust stem and root development.

Now that we've talked in depth about the advantages and are familiar with the right time to repot your seedlings now. Let me walk you through the procedure.

FOUR-STEP REPOTTING PROCEDURE:

1. Gather Resources:

Assemble immaculate 4-inch pots and superior-quality, pre-moistened potting mix. The selection of potting mix is significantly important for uniform moisture dissemination. If multiple seedlings cohabit in a pot, some horticulturists opt to trim surplus seedlings, while others repot them together if done before root binding. You can go with either approach.

2. Extract Seedlings:

Hydrate seedlings to loosen the potting mix, and if utilizing newspaper pots, unfurl them. The matured roots should remain untangled. Delicately remove seedlings, ensuring the roots retain moisture.

3. Isolate Seedlings:

Manage seedlings by their leaves, sidestepping harm to fragile stems. Tactfully pull and jiggle each seedling to separate them, permitting the damp potting mix to adhere to the roots, shielding them from desiccation.

4. Potting Procedure:

Position a seedling in each pot, burying the stem up to its lowest set of leaves. Center the seedling, fill the pot with pre-moistened potting mix, and gently pat it to stabilize the seedling. Water until drainage transpires, replicating the process for remaining seedlings.

After you have transplanted your tomato plant, you cannot treat it like an ordinary plant in your garden as it needs extra care. So, how to care for a transplant?

CARING FOR TRANSPLANTS:

For optimal acclimatization, expose the transplanted seedlings to diffused light or partially cloudy conditions initially, diminishing the likelihood of transplant shock.

It's time to provide them the VIP treatment!

Avoid excessive watering, maintaining the potting soil scarcely moist to forestall waterlogged conditions. Feeding with organic fertilizer, such as liquid fish and seaweed emulsion or granular vegetable fertilizer, establishes the groundwork for vigorous growth.

In short, repotting your tomato seedlings is a procedure that will exploit the plant's distinct rooting capabilities, guaranteeing a sturdy and whole-some base for robust growth, nutrient assimilation, and steadiness upon eventual outdoor transplantation.

If you'd ask how my experience was, following this knowledge, I would say it was awesome.

I embraced the simplicity of sowing seeds directly into the garden. Armed with enthusiasm, I carefully monitored soil temperatures, ensuring they cozied up between 65 and 85ºF (18 and 29 ºC).

To pamper my tomato babies, I generously incorporated compost into the soil, providing them with a nutrient-rich playground. Spacing them 2 feet apart, I gave each seed its breathing room for a glorious journey to adulthood. Anticipating their upward growth, I planted stakes straight away, safeguarding delicate roots from future entanglements.

Results?

I got a lot of vibrant juicy tomatoes.

But there is more to the story. Taking care of soil temperature and apparent conditions of the plant isn't enough. The next chapter unveils the hidden world where nutrients contribute to your tomato plants' growth.

Continue reading, so that your tomatoes not only germinate but develop into fruitful wonders.

Chapter Four

What Your Tomato Plant is Telling You About the Soil

"Food is only as healthy as the soil in which it is grown." – Anne Gibson

Ever thought why do gardeners need fertilizers?

Adding nutrients to the soil is one of the reasons. Fertilizers play an important role in maintaining the pH of the soil.

So, what is soil pH?

H indicates the level of acidity or alkalinity present in the soil. You might be wondering why it is important to consider the pH of the soil. It's because optimal pH ensures plants absorb nutrients efficiently for healthy growth and development.

Let's say you miss out this step and do not adjust the pH of your soil. What can possibly happen?

If the soil is more acidic, plants may struggle to absorb essential nutrients. On the other hand, alkaline soil can cause nutrient imbalances and affect plant health.

thought bubble: *Yeah, I felt like a tightrope walker too when I learned this!*

So, pH of the soil can play an important role in the overall growth of your plant. In order to adjust the pH of your soil, you should first know it's pH.

How to find it?

Let's learn.

Testing Your Soil

In the intricate world beneath our gardens lie different soil types, each with its unique characteristics. Sandy loam, a coveted type, offers an ideal environment for tomatoes with its balanced texture. Understanding your soil type becomes paramount as it directly impacts plant health and growth. This is where soil testing steps into the gardening spotlight. By assessing your soil, you gain insights into its composition, allowing tailored care for your tomatoes. And the role of pH in your plant's growth is crucial too as it influences nutrient availability. Optimal pH levels, between 5.8 to 7.0, ensure your tomatoes can absorb nutrients effectively, fostering healthy development. Before we discuss pH in detail, let's learn how to find out what type of soil you have.

WHAT SOIL TYPE DO YOU HAVE?

One of the easiest ways to find out the type of soil you have is the use of the Jar Test. How is it done?

thought bubble: *I am letting you in on this top secret that A LOT of geological technicians don't know about. (Alright, maybe they do know!)*

Let's see a brief step by step guide to the jar test.

Step 1: Grab a clear jar, a pen, a ruler, a watch, and a sieve or colander.

Step 2: Use the sieve to remove junk from the soil.

Step 3: Put soil in the jar, filling it about a third.

Step 4: Pour water with a teaspoon of dishwashing detergent in the jar, leaving some space at the top.

Step 5: Close the jar, shake it a lot until the soil is all mixed

Step 6: Put the jar down and wait one minute. The heavy sand will go to the bottom.

Step 7: Mark the jar where the sand layer ends. This is after two hours.

Step 8: Leave it alone for 48 hours. Mark where the silt layer ends.

Step 9: Keep waiting for another 48 hours. Mark where the clay layer ends.

Step 10: Use the ruler to measure each layer's height and the total height.

Step 11: Use math to figure out the percentage of sand, silt, and clay.

Step 12: Look at the triangle picture. Put your percentages on it.

Step 13: Where the lines meet on the triangle is your soil type. If it's in the loam area, you have loamy soil.

Step 14: Understand what your soil type means for things like water, nutrients, and how packed it is.

Step 15: Most soils need help. Add things like compost to make it hold more nutrients, drain better, and not get too packed.

JAR OF WATER TEST

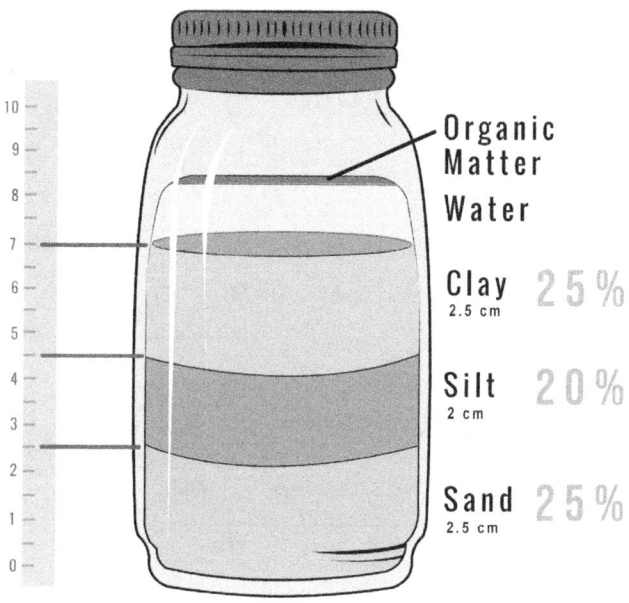

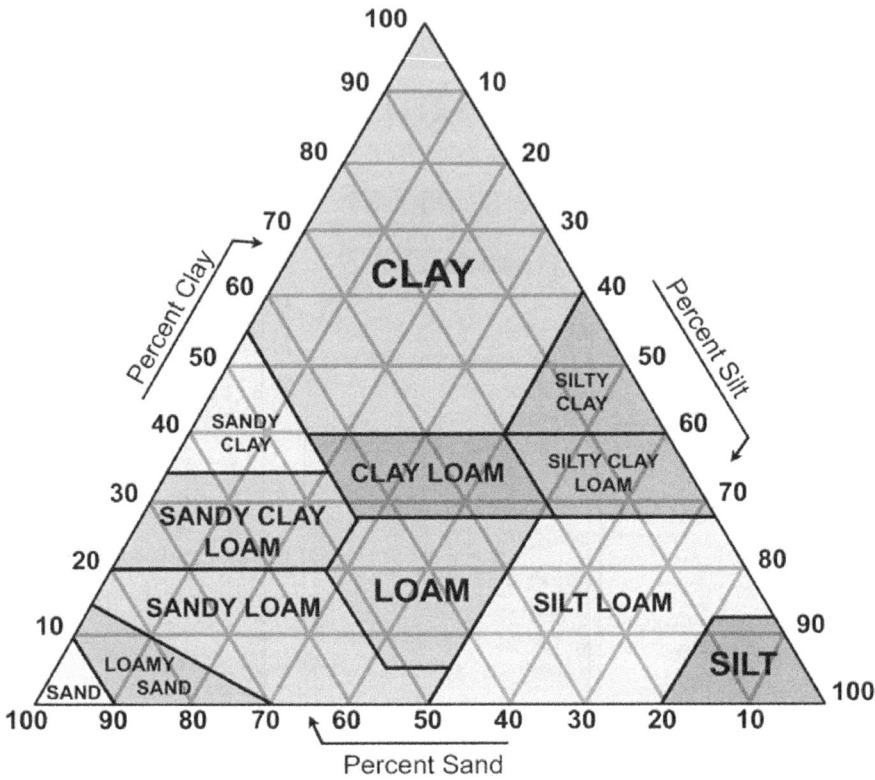

This may be a little intimidating but ponder for a while

Now that you've read the process to figure out what kind of soil you have, let's move on to something equally important—checking how acidic or basic it is.

Now, my dear fellow gardeners, is the time to dig deeper!

Digging a bit deeper to understand the chemical stuff that influences successful gardening and keeping our environment balanced can help you to become better at gardening. To check your garden soil's pH, follow these easy steps:

Step 1: Get What You Need

Grab 2 tablespoons of soil, a bowl, distilled water, vinegar, and baking soda.

Step 2: Check for Acidic Soil

Put 2 tablespoons of soil in a bowl, add distilled water, and sprinkle ½ cup of baking soda. If it fizzes, your soil is acidic.

Step 3: Test for Alkaline Soil

Put 2 tablespoons of soil in a bowl and pour ½ cup vinegar. If it fizzes, your soil is alkaline.

Step 3.5: Take a rest

Run to the living room and fall on the couch.

Step 4: Analyze the results

Very high or low pH can harm plants. A pH of 7 is neutral, and plants like it between 5.5 and 7 for optimal nutrient absorption.

Step 5: Fixing pH

Combat acidic soil with finely ground limestone, and for alkaline soil, use ground sulfur. When adding stuff to your soil, especially near wooded areas, watch out for invasive species like the Asian jumping worm in certain mulches.

Test soil pH every 3 to 5 years for healthy plant growth. Do it in fall for adjustments before spring planting.

Different plants like different pH levels. Knowing your soil pH helps you pick suitable plants or make needed changes.

In short, testing your soil's pH is vital for a healthy garden. ***thought bubble:*** *(Be sure to give it good grades while you mark the test)*. Understanding pH lets you choose the right plants and make adjustments, creating an environment where your plants can thrive.

How to Fertilize Your Soil

If you want to enable successful tomato growth, supplying vital nutrients to fulfill the plant's substantial requirements can be essential. Tomatoes, acknowledged as nutrient-demanding plants, require appropriate fertilization for optimal development.

So, let's learn how to do it the right way. In this section, we will grasp the fundamental characteristics of tomato fertilizer, learn about the variety of options available, and understand the correct methods of application as they are crucial for a fruitful tomato yield.

Fundamental Properties of Tomato Fertilizer:

Did you know that tomato crops rely on three primary elements—nitrogen, phosphorus, and potassium, in addition to diverse trace elements?

Fertilizers amalgamate these components, with their proportions indicated on the packaging. For instance, a 10-10-10 fertilizer signifies an equal distribution of nitrogen, phosphorus, and potassium. If you have conducted a soil examination and are aware of the specific nutrient requirements and pH levels of your soil, it will become easy to select a fertilizer.

Categories of Tomato Fertilizer:

Various types of fertilizers accommodate individual preferences. These include foliar sprays, liquid or soluble alternatives, granular or pelletized compositions, and organic soil enhancements like compost, manure, and alfalfa meal. Each category involves a distinct method of application, with the selection often influenced by factors such as convenience and organic inclinations.

There's no offense in being a little diplomatic in your garden too!

Find a middle ground between organic and inorganic choices to comprehensively enrich your soil with nutrients and maintain the right pH.

Fertilization Approaches:

Incorporate well-decomposed manure into the soil, rich in nutrients but potentially deficient in phosphorus during the planting process.

Other fertilizers require careful consideration of the nitrogen (N), phosphorus (P), and potassium (K) ratio. So, if you want to avoid nutrient imbalances, it is advisable to refrain from excessive fertilization. For side-dressing tomatoes every three to four weeks throughout the season, you can create a shallow trench around the plant and administer fertilizer away from the stem.

And if you are using water-soluble fertilizers that are ideal for tomatoes cultivated in containers, you can administer them every one to two weeks.

Understanding soil fertility is pivotal for fostering sturdy tomato plants, irrespective of the cultivation space, whether you have an extensive garden or a compact balcony. This awareness will guarantee you the provision of essential nutrients for the robust growth and bountiful harvests of tomatoes.

THE MAGIC OF COMPOST TEA

Producing compost tea is a simple method that results in an outstanding universal plant nourishment, enhancing both plant well-being and soil vigor.

thought bubble: *Even if your plants are coffee connoisseurs, you should serve them compost tea.*

Its benefits are tried and tested.

This nutrient-abundant mixture is crafted from mature compost, marked by organic elements completing decomposition, ensuring a combination of major and minor nutrients imperative for plant development. You can use compost tea not only for your young plants but also as a revitalizing potion for more established ones.

The formula for compost tea is very simple. Essentially, it requires situating compost in water and letting it steep for seven to ten days, contingent on the compost-to-water ratio. The sign that the tea is prepared is the alteration of the water's color to a tea-like hue. Once formulated, you can use the compost tea by pouring it around the base of plants every two weeks or administering it to plant leaves as a foliar spray.

Compost tea mimics the nutrient constitution of compost itself, enveloping major nutrients such as nitrogen, phosphorus, and potassium (NPK) in nearly identical proportions alongside various minor nutrients. The liquid nature of compost tea expedites the accessibility of these nutrients to plant roots, ensuring swift fertilization compared to arid alternatives requiring interaction with soil water.

Beyond nurturing plants, compost tea nurtures the health of soil microorganisms involved in decomposing organic matter into plant nutrients. Concurrently, these microorganisms combat detrimental fungi, offering protection against ailments like powdery mildew, downy mildew, and botrytis.

Implementing compost tea involves varied methods, providing flexibility in its formulation. One technique involves a "tea bag" method, enclosing compost in a burlap sack submerged in water. Another straightforward approach entails filling a receptacle with compost and water, allowing the amalgamation to settle for a week to ten days. Additionally, a "bucket in a barrel" tactic utilizes an aged plastic or tin container filled with compost, suspended in a larger water barrel, providing a convenient brewing solution.

Compost tea can also function as a foliar spray by filtering the solution through cheesecloth into a sprayer, delivering the advantages directly to plant leaves and stems. This application serves as a fungicide, with the microorganisms in the tea combating fungi responsible for diverse foliar diseases.

If you successfully integrate compost tea into your routine gardening practices, it would be as if you add mature compost into the soil, enriching soil quality and its capacity to retain water.

thought bubble: *In no time, your plants will not only turn into tea connoisseurs.*

The versatile benefits of compost tea establish it as a valuable asset for both plant and soil health, embodying a comprehensive approach to gardening.

79

And with that you've completed this chapter! You've learned how to decipher fertilizer labels, test soil for optimal conditions, and even whip up the nutrient-rich magic of compost tea.

Soil isn't the only thing tomato plants need. It sounds simple to water plants but it's one area that so many people get wrong, even killing with kindness as they drown their plants. Fortunately, there are a few systems that can help us keep on top of this. Let's learn about the secrets of watering the plants the right way in the next chapter.

Chapter Five

The Fine Art of Watering Tomato Plants

Watering your tomatoes is just like cooking your favorite dish. You have to be very careful while adding the ingredients. Right proportions matter a lot. More or less proportions can totally change the taste. In this chapter, you'll learn to water your tomatoes so you don't overwater or underwater your plants.

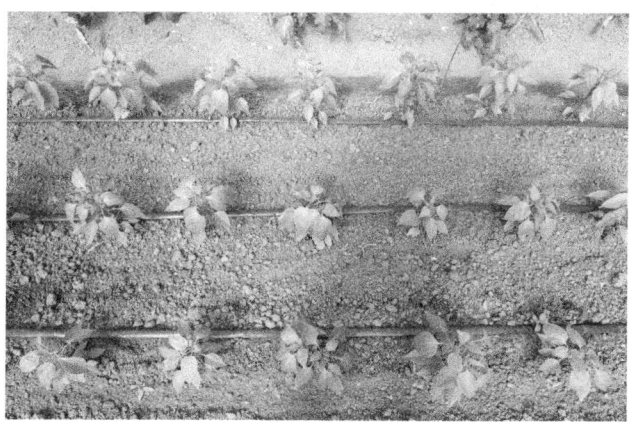

While watering plants, take time to talk to them! Studies have shown that talking to tomato plants encourages growth, with female voices encouraging a whole inch more growth than those plants with a male voice. Fun Fact, it was Charles Darwin's great-great-granddaughter who got the best results with her tomato plant, growing a whole 2 inches.

Isn't it interesting?

Now, let's explore more about watering tomatoes.

How Much Water Do Tomato Plants Need

If you are planning to grow tomatoes from seeds, you should know that the soil may rapidly dehydrate because seedlings need a lot of nutrients. They are typically housed in compact containers or trays.

thought bubble: *It's like there's a who-will-blindly-gobble-and-gulp-more contest going on between them*

So, you might need to check the soil daily to ensure it hasn't dried.

How much water do you think seedlings require?

These baby plants need a very little amount of water. So, while watering the seedlings, use a spray bottle to gently dampen the seedlings. Make sure that you maintain moisture primarily at the soil's surface.

If you feel that the soil has become excessively saturated, relocate the seedlings to an area with enhanced air circulation and postpone watering until necessary.

thought bubble: *Avoid letting the seedlings linger in a pool of water. You haven't invited them out of their seeds to attend a pool party!*

As the seedlings start to emerge and develop, their water requirements will obviously increase. So, if you notice that the soil in the tray dries within a day, it may be time to transfer your seedlings to the garden or a larger receptacle.

Tomatoes level up!

In the initial stages of the growing season, irrigate the plants each morning. However, if the temperatures rise, you might need to water your tomato plants two times daily.

Generally, garden tomatoes need approximately 1 to 2 inches of water on a weekly basis.

Interestingly, tomato plants cultivated in pots necessitate a greater amount of water compared to tomatoes in the garden. Why? The soil within containers warms up rapidly, resulting in increased evaporation.

If you are growing tomatoes in containers, I've got an important tip for you.

Irrigate the plants until water flows freely from the base. Water in the morning, and reassess soil moisture levels in the afternoon. If the soil seems dry approximately 1 inch beneath the surface, it's time to irrigate once more.

But if you're growing tomatoes in the garden, how do you water your plants?

You can't obviously use a spray bottle for the plants in your garden.

So, what are the available options?

FOUR IRRIGATION SYSTEMS TO KEEP PLANTS MOIST

When irrigating your tomato plants, there are different approaches you can experiment with. But the most important thing is ensuring that you hydrate them well. Just do not pull them out, dip them in water, and plant them back. It is not an option.

Watering can

If you want to use a watering can to irrigate your plants, selecting one with a rose spout can yield better outcomes. It's because a spout distributes water in multiple smaller streams, as opposed to a single large flow. This is also preferable as an overly forceful stream can disturb the soil necessary for the plant's ongoing, consistent growth.

Hose

If you decide on using a hose for irrigating your tomato plants, use a nozzle or watering wand to facilitate a gradual and gentle water release because you might not want the fast flowing water to wash the soil.

Drip irrigation:

A drip irrigation system stands out as among the most efficient approaches to hydrate tomato plants. In this technique, water passes through petite tubes positioned at the plant base, ensuring direct delivery to the roots.

Another advantage it can provide your garden is its facilitation of uniform water distribution among all tomato plants.

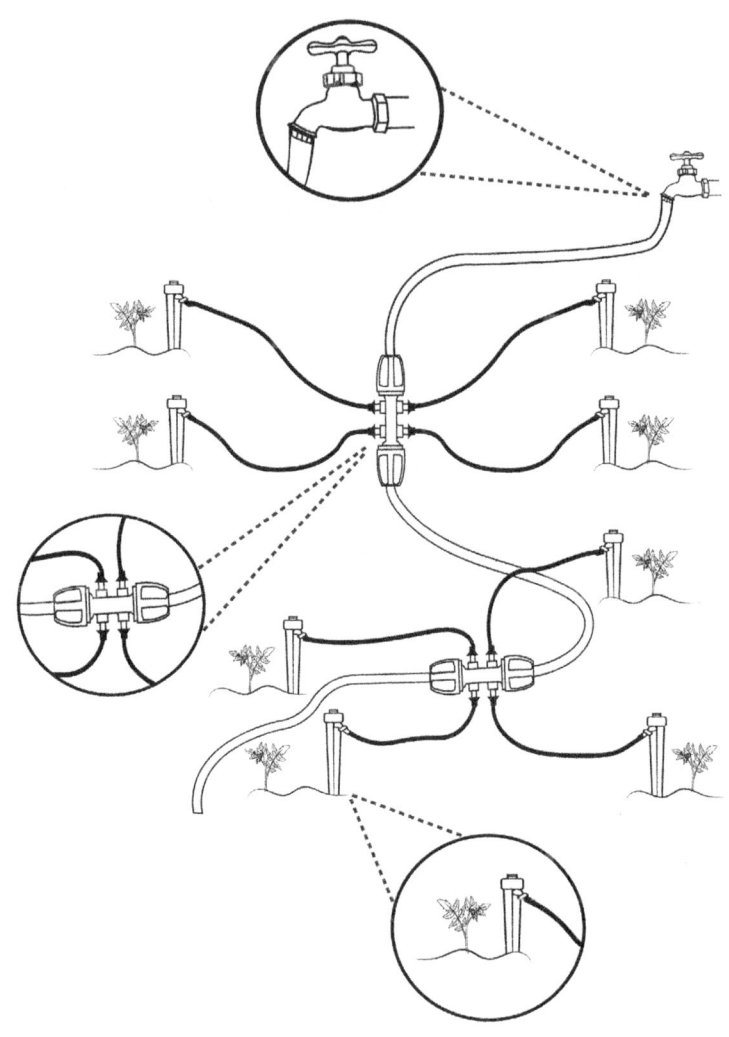

This diagram gives you the general idea. Of course, it's not to scale

Some of the components. Image Courtesy of Carpathen.com

Sprinkler:

While a sprinkler might seem like a convenient choice for hydrating tomato plants, it ranks as the least desirable option. Sprinklers disperse water from above, reaching the leaves and elevating the risk of diseases and pests harming your tomatoes. Additionally, the moisture evaporates swiftly, depriving your plants of the essential water they require for optimal growth.

Furthermore, directing a sprinkler to a specific area proves challenging, potentially resulting in watering other plants simultaneously. This could lead to issues such as weed growth or overwatering other crops you intend to cultivate.

Speaking of overwatering plants, how do you tell if your plant isn't getting the right amount of water?

thought bubble: *Your plants might start dropping hints like melodramatic actors in a soap opera. To pick up on those cues, you might need to keep a close eye on them.*

Let's find out.

SIGNS YOUR TOMATO PLANT ISN'T GETTING THE RIGHT AMOUNT OF WATER

Sufficient water is crucial for the robust development of tomato plants, yet an excess can be harmful.

Why?

It's because an abundance of water displaces air from the soil around the plant's roots, leading to root suffocation and eventual demise. Strangely, the outcomes of both overwatering and underwatering manifest similarly, with wilting, yellowing, browning, and leaf loss. Various diseases and pests can also imitate the symptoms of overwatering.

So, how do you know if you've overwatered or underwatered your plants.

Signs of Overwatered Tomato Plants

thought bubble: *When it comes to watering, your tomato garden might start to feel like a suspenseful movie, but with more soil and less popcorn!*

So, when tomato plants are provided with more water than they can effectively absorb, apparent changes in the plant and the adjacent soil can be seen. Initial indications of overwatering in tomato plants include fissured fruit and anomalies like blisters or bumps on the lower leaves. If the excessive watering persists, the leaf abnormalities progress to a corky texture.

In addition to this excessive watering can cause the roots to undergo submersion, decay, and rot, leading to a diminished water supply for the remaining section of the plant.

Withering and discoloration can occur to the leaves and stems, culminating in the complete collapse and demise of the entire plant. Indicators of potential overwatering in tomato plants include persistent puddles on the soil surface hours after watering or a spongy feel to the soil upon touch.

How to Save an Overwatered Tomato Plant

Taking the right measures at the right time can aid in the revival of a tomato plant that has been overwatered, enabling it to subsequently flourish.

thought bubble: *Much like a superhero armed with a watering can, swooping in to rescue a tomato plant so they get a second chance to conquer the salad universe.*

If your potted plant is affected, extract it and delicately remove damp compost devoid of roots. Position the root zone on a couple of newspapers to facilitate the removal of surplus moisture. Plant it back again. With proper care, tomato plants can show speedy recovery, often yielding visible improvements within just one to two weeks.

To completely avoid the risk of overwatering the tomato plant, place it in a container equipped with drainage holes that snugly accommodate the roots, filling any voids with new compost.

If your plant is growing in soil and the excessive amount of water results from extended, intense rainfall, here's what you can do. Delicately cover the plant with a transparent plastic sheet. You can support the sheet with dried branches. You can then lift the plastic sheet once the rain subsides.

This will lower the risk of overwatering.

The wise quote "prevention is better than cure" is accurate beyond all reason. Speaking of it, let's learn about the right amount of water to use while irrigating your plants so we don't have to worry about fixing the overwatered or underwatered plants in the first place.

Correct Watering for Tomato Plants

The rule of thumb: While your tomato seedlings recently transplanted to the garden might necessitate consistently damp soil, mature plants only need watering when the soil dries to a depth of 2 to 3 inches.

Water tomato plants in the morning, refraining from moistening the leaves to deter fungal leaf ailments. Vigorous tomato plants thrive with approximately 1 inch of weekly water, a requirement that can most probably be fulfilled by rainfall. (TOMATOES JUST LIKE TO KEEP IT ORGANIC)

A substantial rainfall lasting three or four hours is typically sufficient for your plants for the whole week. However, in hot, arid, and windy conditions, your plants may require daily watering.

But if you are still unsure about when to hydrate your tomato plants, here's a tip for you.

Insert a trowel into the soil 4 or 5 inches from the stem base and assess moisture levels. You can irrigate only if the soil feels dry to the touch at a depth of 2 to 3 inches.

Saving Under Watered Tomatoes

As mentioned before, tomatoes exhibit identical signs in both under watering and over watering scenarios. Leaf wilting starts and is accompanied by yellowing and curling at the tips and margins. The fruit fails to harden, and the soil becomes rigid to the touch.

Noticing these symptoms? Rush and grab your watering can before it's too late!

If you've been using a drip irrigation system, water might accumulate in drip trays. The initial step is to quickly remove this stagnant water. The accumulation of water inhibits root absorption and contributes to keeping your tomato plants inadequately watered.

This accumulation can affect outdoor plants too. So, make sure to dismantle any automated irrigation system you may have set up. Opting for manual watering is the most secure choice. If the soil mix is the problem, try replanting or transferring your tomatoes into improved soil and employ mulch to regulate moisture levels within the potting mix.

The right amount of water can help you achieve your desired bright tomato fruits.

thought bubble: *Afterall, we're aiming for the big and juicy tomatoes attracting more attention than a cat video on the internet!*

As your tomato plants flourish, their robust growth signals the need for support. In the upcoming chapter, we'll delve into the art of training them to thrive on a trellis. Additionally, we'll explore techniques for judiciously pruning tomatoes, ensuring not only their sustained health but also maximizing fruit production. Stay tuned for valuable insights into nurturing your garden bounty.

Please Leave a Review

Recall the adventure I shared with you in the introduction? My commitment now is to guide as many people as possible away from the potential pitfalls of starting their tomato-growing journey. Encountering one or more setbacks can be disheartening, possibly even discouraging. Yet, I implore you to persist and recognize that success is undoubtedly within reach.

Countless individuals aspire to cultivate their own food, with growing tomatoes high on their list of desires. The allure lies in savoring vibrant flavors, envisioning reduced grocery expenses, and aiming to provide healthier meals for their families. Unfortunately, one misstep may crumble that cherished dream.

Drawing from my own gardening experience, I recognize the significance of obtaining information that aligns with your current level of expertise. This is pivotal for attaining success in gardening. My commitment is unwavering to ensuring that a broad spectrum of individuals finds the guidance that resonates with them. The pleasure of indulging in weekly pasta nights, enhanced by the exquisite flavor of freshly harvested tomatoes, should be accessible to everyone, and my goal is to turn this aspiration into a tangible reality.

However, I'll need your assistance.

Without the insights of gardeners who have tried my methods, this book could be as bad as those dreaded videos on YouTube. It might slip past the eyes of those who need it the most.

By leaving a review of this book on Amazon, you can stop that from happening. You can show other readers that this is a trusted resource.

By sharing a review of this book on Amazon, you can prevent that from happening. Your review can demonstrate to other readers that this is a reliable resource.

In just a few sentences, you can inform fellow novice gardeners how this book aided you and what they can anticipate discovering inside. Your words will guide them toward the advice they're seeking without a wilted tomato in sight!

Thank you for your contribution. A book is genuinely nothing without its readers.

bit.ly/3VqePiV

Chapter Six

Techniques to Support Tomato Plant Growth

T he support of a tomato plant more than holds up its heavy fruit. Providing support means the plant has better access to the sun and less exposure to soil-borne diseases. This impacts your yield. A staked plant can produce an average of 8 pounds of tomatoes whereas one that has been trained on a trellis can produce between 12 and 20 pounds!

Supporting a plant can therefore have huge benefits for your tomato garden.

Let's learn how to prune your tomatoes and provide them the support they need to thrive.

WHY TOMATO PLANTS NEED PRUNING

As we've discussed in previous chapters, tomatoes fall into two main groups: determinate and indeterminate.

Determinate tomatoes reach a specific size and cease growing, while indeterminate tomatoes persist in growth throughout the entire season.

Pruning can benefit indeterminate tomatoes the most. I can practically hear you asking WHY? Hang tight; you're about to find your answers.

Picture this: there's a tomato plant and they have got a nutrient supply in the soil. Unfortunately, the nutrient supply isn't infinite. Instead, it is limited. But the plant needs all the nutrients to get juicy tomato fruits.

But the little pirates invade. These are the tiny leaves at the base of the plant and can suck all the nutrients preventing it from reaching the parts of the plant that actually needs them. This can result in retarded growth of the lovely tomato plant.

You might not appreciate these little pirates taking the nutrients your tomatoes deserve, right? Therefore, what you can do is detach these little leaflets from the plant.

Tomatoes rescued!

And not only can you save your tomatoes but can help them thrive.

To sum up, pruning indeterminate tomatoes enhances fruit yield by eliminating surplus growth that sucks energy away from fruit development. The removal of excess growth redirects energy towards the fruits and diminishes shading, accelerating the maturation of the fruits.

It's a win-win!

But the benefits of pruning do not end here. There's more to it.

It also facilitates increased air circulation within a plant, decreasing humidity and hastening the drying of any lingering leaves. This less moist environment is less conducive to developing fungal and bacterial diseases.

Excited to start pruning your tomatoes for maximum results? Let's do it!

A Guide to Pruning Tomatoes

Tomatoes act as solar-powered energy factories. In their initial weeks in the garden, preceding the appearance of blossoms, tomato plants channel their energy into the growth of fresh leaves. Subsequently, additional branches arise to accommodate more leaves.

What happens next is a lateral stem sprouts directly from the primary stem, while suckers are new branches that emerge from the main stem, just above a leaf branch or lateral stem.

thought bubble: Think of it like the tomato plant's version of a family reunion: the main stem is the cool grandparent, the lateral stem is the eccentric cousin who starts breakdancing, and the suckers are the mischievous siblings photobombing the family portrait.

As tomato plants enlarge, their leaves generate even more energy, explaining why they persist in producing stems and suckers throughout the season. Suckers emerging in the mid to late season are typically feeble, yield subpar fruit, and deplete energy from the primary stem.

Additionally, suckers near the base of the plant exhibit greater strength compared to those higher up, as the plant's sugar concentration diminishes with increasing height.

You might not want the suckers to pour water on your efforts to grow healthy tomato plants. So, let's use the different types of pruning to fight the suckers.

Basic pruning

Pruning tomato sucker shoots when they are in their initial and tender stage is more beneficial than waiting for the sucker to mature and gain strength.

How to do it?

Gently grip the base of the sucker between your thumb and forefinger. Pinch it to break it off or delicately flex the sucker back and forth until it breaks. This method is referred to as "basic pruning."

Pinch young suckers with your fingers rather than clippers or a knife. Pinched injuries heal faster and pose fewer risks of disease in young plants.

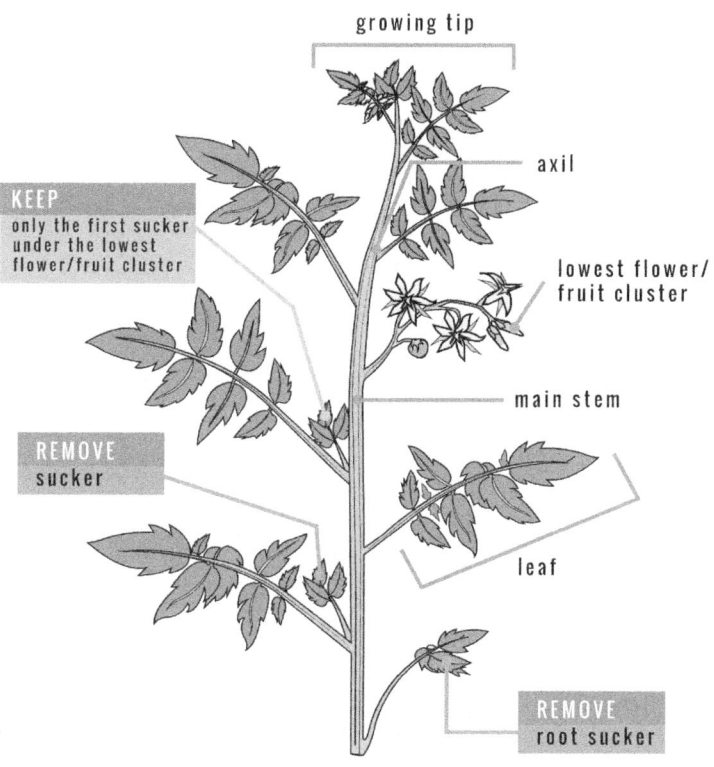

growing tip

axil

KEEP
only the first sucker
under the lowest
flower/fruit cluster

lowest flower/
fruit cluster

REMOVE
sucker

main stem

leaf

REMOVE
root sucker

Detach the little leaflet suckers from the plant

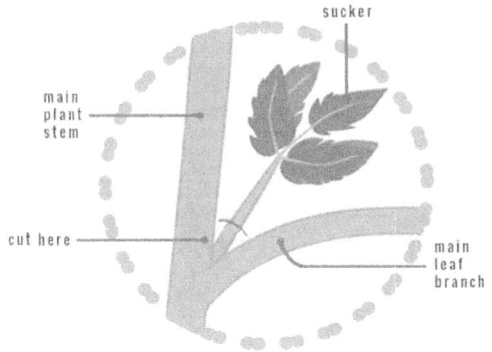

Here's a closer look

*Pinch it to break it off or delicately flex
the sucker back and forth until it breaks*

As stems age and toughen, you may find it necessary to use garden clippers instead of fingers on mature plants.

Make sure to disinfect your tools to prevent infections in the tomato plant.

For optimal strength in your tomato plant, trim side stems beneath the initial fruit cluster. As your tomato plant matures, its lower leaves will exhibit a yellow hue. Pinch or prune the yellowed leaves to thwart diseases, enhance the visual appeal of the tomato plant, and assist the plant in maintaining its energy concentration on fruit production.

Remember, excess of everything is bad!

If you cultivate tomatoes in a hot region, refrain from over-pruning. Excessive sunlight or prolonged, intense exposure can result in tomatoes developing sunscald.

thought bubble: *However, you can over-prune once the scientists come up with a sunscreen for your tomatoes!*

Missouri pruning

An alternative to simple pruning for trimming suckers involves pinching them off at the tips rather than the base of the shoot. By leaving a few leaves, you enable the plant to generate more energy for ripening tomatoes while providing shade to maturing fruit. This method is referred to as "Missouri pruning."

Missouri pruning mitigates shock to the plant, proving especially beneficial in hot, sunny climates or when suckers have grown substantial.

The Missouri technique of pruning

The drawback of Missouri pruning is that the remaining suckers may generate new ones.

thought bubble: *It's like the 'Whack-a-Mole' game; you trim one sucker, and two more pop up, playing botanical hide-and-seek.*

So, you should exercise careful vigilance over plants when opting to prune only the tips of suckers.

Root pruning

Certain gardeners opt to fortify tomato plants by engaging in root pruning. This involves cutting the roots, disrupting the plant's growth cycle, and inducing enough stress to prompt a more accelerated maturation than it would naturally undergo.

It might require attention to detail, and as a beginner, you can skip this.

The right moment for root pruning is as the initial clusters of tomatoes begin to ripen. Introduce a long kitchen knife, pitchfork, or spade a few inches away from the plant's base, penetrating the soil to a depth of 8 to 10 inches. Execute your cut around the plant, ensuring it's only halfway through.

You can also "top" your tomatoes. Approximately a month before the final frost, use a high-quality pair of garden pruners to trim the top of the plant's terminal shoot above the last blossom. This method, known as "topping the plant," enables the optimal allocation of nutrients to the fruit, enhancing production towards the end of your crop. Topping your plant increases the likelihood of a final harvest comprising red tomatoes rather than green ones.

Topping the plant method provides a better chance of producing red tomatoes

Now that we have discussed the method of pruning and the major types of pruning let's explore the different types of support for tomato plants.

Different Supports for Tomato Plants

Supports help plants stay strong and prevent stems from breaking in the wind. It also keeps the fruit off the ground and helps the sunlight to reach the entire plant. Offering adequate support aids in their robust growth, ensuring intact stems and keeping the fruits elevated, preventing contact with the ground. It not only provides safeguarding against unintended harm and adverse weather conditions but also aids in minimizing tomato diseases by preventing overcrowding and maintaining a sufficient distance between the plants. Besides, employing various types of tomato supports can simplify the harvesting process.

Instead of lifting and shifting plants to locate lower fruits, the fruits are readily accessible, typically at a more convenient picking height.

thought bubble: It's the lazy gardener's dream come true – no need for acrobatics or interpretive dance moves just to pluck a tomato!

Almost uncountable benefits! So, what is stopping you from optimizing the yield?

The most common methods for providing support to tomato plants include:

1. Trellis
2. Cages
3. Wires and strings
4. Stakes

Are you wondering which one to opt for?

Several crucial factors come into play when deciding how to provide support for your tomato plants. Initial consideration should be given to your surroundings. The area in which you reside and the specific location for growing tomatoes typically determine the most suitable support method.

Assess the wind conditions at your site and evaluate the likelihood of disturbance from human or animal activities affecting the tomato plants.

Additionally, it's essential to consider the variety of tomatoes you're cultivating. Pay attention to the characteristics of the tomatoes a plant will yield, considering whether they are suitable for salads, canning, or cooking. For example, larger beefsteak tomatoes typically demand greater support compared to varieties with smaller fruits.

thought bubble: And no, I'm not discriminating against tomatoes, it's just a matter of co-mato-on sense (ouch!)

Another factor to consider is whether the type or types you cultivate are determinate or indeterminate.

Determinate tomato varieties follow a restricted growth pattern, necessitating considerably less support, making them well-suited for container cultivation.

On the other hand, indeterminate varieties will persist in growth and fruit formation for an extended duration, often resulting in more substantial plants that generally demand increased support.

A vertical growth approach facilitated by a trellis can help conserve space when cultivating tomatoes against a wall or fence. However, standalone trellises can be fashioned for nearly any cultivation area.

Cages serve as independent solutions adaptable to various locations, providing comprehensive protection by enclosing tomato plants from all sides.

Cordon cultivation is frequently regarded as an optimal space-saving resolution, while simple stakes may also fulfill a comparable function in specific environments.

In this section, we'll explore different types of trellis to support the tomato plants.

Different types of tomato trellis are available in the market. So, if you don't want to spend time making your own trellis, you can purchase it.

Opting for a do-it-yourself strategy, on the other hand, can present various advantages. Crafting your trellis allows you to adopt a more environmentally friendly approach, utilizing natural or repurposed materials that might have otherwise been discarded.

YOUR GARDEN TRELLIS: WHERE VEGETABLES GO TO HANG OUT STYL-
ISHLY!

Here are some intriguing do-it-yourself trellis ideas that you might want to
use:

Natural Branch Trellis

An economical method to craft your trellis involves using natural branches
from your garden. Interweave them and secure them with natural twine,
creating trellises of various shapes and sizes.

Sporting a rustic and organic appearance, these trellises can enhance the
aesthetic of your kitchen garden. Moreover, crafting them will be virtually
cost-free and won't present disposal concerns when they reach the end of
their utility. It's a win-win!

Bamboo Trellis

If you cultivate bamboo in your garden, you can leverage the canes for
various purposes. Utilize bamboo canes to craft a trellis for supporting
tomatoes. Similar to the natural branch concept mentioned earlier, bamboo canes can be easily fastened together with natural twine to fashion
diverse trellis patterns.

Wood Trellis

Repurposed wood pieces can be employed similarly to form a lattice or
ladder structure, providing support for your tomato plants.

Pallet Wood Trellis

For a more robust trellis, reusing pallet wood proves especially beneficial. Pallet wood trellises exhibit significant strength, making them ideal not just for tomato plants but also for supporting squash, pumpkins, and other climbing plants in your cultivation.

thought bubble: *Let your plants make the ultimate fashion statement with pallet wood trellis!*

Chicken Wire Trellis

If you have leftover chicken wire, affixing a segment within a basic wooden frame can offer a quick do-it-yourself trellis solution for supporting your tomato plants.

Livestock Panel Trellis

Reusing an aged livestock panel or a section of fencing can be reused into a simple yet robust trellis for your tomato plants.

Positioned vertically or leaned against a fence, these metal fencing sections can provide the necessary support for your tomato plants as they mature.

Pipe Trellis

Leftover pipes from a home plumbing project might prove valuable in your vegetable garden. While old pipes are commonly reused for constructing hoop house frames in new greenhouses, you can also utilize them to craft a trellis for your plants.

Bicycle Wheel Trellis

Secure a few discarded bicycle wheels against the structure; their spokes serve as excellent anchor points for fastening growing tomato plants. Additionally, the entire arrangement can double as a whimsical piece of garden artwork.

thought bubble: *As the proverb goes, the unique-y wheels get the grease.*

Fishing Net Trellis

Reusing old fishing nets can prevent wildlife entanglement and the common occurrence of them washing up on beaches. Drape them over walls or fences or spread them within a wooden frame. This not only offers support for tomatoes and other plants but also enables you to contribute to addressing plastic pollution.

Securing your growing tomato plants to the trellis using natural twine aids in maintaining plant structure and promoting robust growth. Additionally, this practice ensures that the fruits are elevated above the ground, facilitating easy harvesting.

HOW TO TRAIN YOUR PLANT

Training your tomato plants is like giving them a little gardening lesson to grow big and strong.

thought bubble: *But contrary to any trainer you have come across in your life, you will be required to go easy on the plants.*

Imagine you're creating a cozy home for your tomatoes to thrive in! So, here's how you can guide your plants:

Step 1: Set Up a Simple Trellis

You can use stakes or bailing wire to create a support system for your tomato buddies. For smaller tomatoes, go for 1-inch by 1-inch by 4-foot stakes every 4 to 6 feet, with twine every 6 inches. If you've got the big guys, try 2-inch-by-2-inch-by-7-foot stakes every 6 to 8 feet, with twine every 12 inches. This helps your tomatoes stand tall and happy.

Step 2: Start Early and Be Gentle

iding your tomatoes about a month after transplanting them. Use gentle ties – think sturdy twine, plant tape, fabric strips, or even recycled pantyhose – to secure the stems to the support structure every 6 or 8 inches. Remember, they're delicate, so be kind!

Step 3: Choose Your Approach

Decide if you want a single stem or multiple stems. For a single stem, go for the single-stake or single-string trellis method. If you're in for multiple stems, the horizontal-string trellis or cage approach is your game. Plan this ahead before planting, as it affects how close your tomatoes should be to each other.

Step 4: Deal with Suckers

Suckers are those little side shoots that pop up between leaves and the main stem. If you're going for a single stem, snap those suckers off as soon as they show up. For multiple stems, let the first suckers grow into their own stems, but trim the later ones. Use your fingers for this – they snap off easily.

Step 5: Keep Pruning

Consistency is key. Keep securing stems to the support structure as they grow, and keep saying bye-bye to those suckers. You're the plant boss!

Step 6: Final Pruning Before Frost

About a month before the first frost, give your plants a little haircut – trim the tips of each stem just above the top fruit cluster. It might seem a bit drastic, but it helps your tomatoes focus their energy on ripening the remaining fruit before winter arrives.

So, there you have it! By training your tomatoes, you're basically ensuring they grow up happy, healthy, and ready to give you delicious fruits.

thought bubble: *We believe in producing Oscar-worthy performances, not just tomatoes! Get ready for a blockbuster harvest – coming soon to a backyard near you!*

As you delve deeper into the journey of nurturing your tomatoes, prepare to have a closer look at the potential challenges nature might throw your way. Despite the solid foundation of soil, water, and support, stay tuned for insights on swift, organic problem-solving. In the next chapter, you'll explore how to protect your plants from pests and diseases without using chemical pesticides.

Chapter Seven

Choosing the Best Moment to Harvest Your Tomatoes and Store Them

"The greatest form of maturity is at harvest time. This is when we must learn how to reap without complaint if the amounts are small and how to reap without apology if the amounts are big." – Jim Rohn

In this chapter, we will address common pitfalls associated with tomato harvesting, emphasizing the significance of timing for optimal nutritional content and flavor. Understanding the mistakes often made during this process is crucial for cultivating a better yield. Additionally, we will provide practical insights into safe storage methods, ensuring the long-term preservation of tomatoes for sustained use.

WHEN AND HOW TO HARVEST TOMATOES

Ideally, the optimal moment to harvest tomatoes is when they reach ripeness on the vine. However, discerning the fruit's ripeness can be tricky. While we often associate ripe tomatoes with a vibrant red hue in stores, the truth is that color isn't a reliable indicator for picking. If you wait until the fruit is uniformly red, it could potentially be past its prime.

thought bubble: *Harvesting tomatoes is like trying to pick the perfect movie on Netflix – if you wait for the right color, you might end up with a tomato that's past its starring role!*

Continue reading to discover the ideal time to harvest tomatoes at their peak.

If you've ever savored a tomato ripened on the vine, straight from the plant, you're aware of its succulent, sweet taste, brimming with that distinctive tomato flavor. Tomatoes found in grocery stores frequently fall short in comparison, and this can be attributed to a couple of factors.

Initially, these tomatoes are frequently packed and transported over long distances. Sending a vine-ripened tomato through this process would probably lead to it reaching its destination in a bruised, battered state, with its delightful juices leaking. Additionally, such tomatoes become vulnerable to fungal diseases, potentially turning them into moldy fruits. Consequently, commercially available tomatoes are harvested when they exhibit only a hint of redness, far from being truly ripe. To induce ripening, they undergo a process involving ethylene gas and are subsequently stored in refrigeration, often maintained below 50°F (10°C), resulting in a less flavorful fruit.

Another factor contributing to underwhelming tomatoes is the selective breeding for specific traits. In supermarket produce, the objective is to deliver the goods to the store swiftly and have them ready for sale before any damage or spoilage occurs. Consequently, farmers seek out varieties with resilient fruit that has been specifically bred for prolonged storage and efficient shipping, prioritizing these characteristics over maximizing flavor.

Tomatoes release a gas. Fully developed, mature green tomatoes generate ethylene gas. Within the mature green tomato, two growth hormones undergo a transformation, leading to the generation of this gas. Subsequently, the gas influences the aging of the fruit's cells, leading to softening and the transition from green to a red hue. Ethylene enhances the presence of carotenoids (red and yellow hues) while diminishing chlorophyll (green color).

Due to this mechanism, tomatoes stand out as one of the few vegetables – I mean, fruits – that can be harvested before reaching full ripeness. Ideally, tomatoes should be picked when they are in the mature green stage and then permitted to ripen off the vine. This approach helps avoid issues like splitting or bruising and affords a certain level of influence over the ripening progression.

Determining the optimal time for harvesting to achieve peak flavor introduces another consideration. If the tomatoes don't appear fully ripe to your observation, but temperatures are rising, and there's a risk of sunscald, it might be advisable to harvest earlier than your preference. The same principle applies in the case of unexpected cold spells. If a freeze becomes imminent, it's wiser to promptly harvest the fruit than to risk potential loss.

Considering all these factors, harvesting tomatoes at the breaker stage offers a few benefits. It diminishes the likelihood of insect harm, is less prone to experiencing radial cracks, and minimizes the fruit's vulnerability to harsh weather conditions that could harm or bruise the fragile skin, potentially leading to disease.

When harvesting tomatoes at the mature green stage, it's crucial to identify the subtle signs. Keep an eye out for the initial faint blush of color. Naturally, you can also gather ripe tomatoes – ripe ones will submerge in water. While vine-ripened tomatoes tend to be the sweetest, certain tomato varieties are too weighty for this method. Hence, opting to pick tomatoes at their mature green stage and letting ethylene gas perpetuate the ripening process.

thought bubble: *Ripening tomatoes is a delicate balance – it's like being a tomato matchmaker navigating the garden dating scene. Some like the slow romance on the vine, while others are all about the whirlwind romance with ethylene. It's a veggie love story with a hint of suspense!*

The method for harvesting tomato fruit is relatively straightforward. Pay close attention to the base of the fruit, particularly for large heirloom varieties, as this is where ripening typically starts. Gently press the fruit to assess its firmness. When the initial hint of red emerges on the tomato's skin, it's almost time for tomato harvest.

After dedicating considerable effort to nurture your tomatoes, it's crucial to avoid haphazardly yanking them from the vine to prevent damage.

Instead, opt for sharp garden snips or shears to precisely cut the stalk just above the calyx, which forms to safeguard the bud.

In the case of tomatoes in the red stage, already at their peak ripeness, and if immediate consumption is intended, you may detach the fruit by gently twisting it away from the stem.

As previously noted, tomatoes continue to ripen post-harvest. Harvesting at the color break stage and refrigerating can prolong the tomato harvest by a few weeks. This halts ethylene production, essentially placing the fruit in a temporary state of dormancy.

Certain gardeners avoid the refrigerator and, instead, arrange the fruit in a solitary layer within cardboard boxes in a dimly lit room or encase each tomato in newspaper or waxed paper. Some cultivators suspend entire plants, a method particularly applicable in the humid East. Alternatively, some individuals merely position tomatoes at the color break stage on the kitchen counter. Regardless of the chosen storage method, it's advisable to inspect the tomatoes every few days for signs of ripening or spoilage. Tomatoes stored at room temperature typically ripen within a span of 5-7 days.

For an accelerated ripening process, expedite the ripening of your tomatoes by placing them in a paper bag along with a banana or other already ripe tomatoes. Both the matured fruit and banana emit ethylene gas, an accelerating agent that speeds up the ripening process.

Green fruit is anticipated to ripen within approximately 2 weeks at temperatures ranging from 65-70°F (18-21°C). If stored at 55°F (13°C), ripening is expected within 3-4 weeks. It's crucial to avoid storing tomatoes below 50°F (14°C) as it leads to the development of tasteless fruit.

Short-Term Tomato Storage

When it comes to storing tomatoes, understanding their ripeness is key to preserving their flavor and texture. Tomatoes, originating in a tropical environment, are best stored at room temperature, emphasizing the importance of fully mature tomatoes. Refrigerating anything other than completely ripe tomatoes can adversely affect flavor, color, and texture, resulting in a grainy consistency.

thought bubble: *Putting unripe tomatoes in the fridge is like sending them to vegetable detention – they come out all cold, flavorless, and with a texture that screams, "I've been in timeout!" It's the icy timeout for tomatoes.*

This principle extends to cherry tomatoes as well. Temperatures below 55°F (13°C), like those in your fridge, impede enzyme activity in unripe tomatoes, affecting flavor development. Even fully ripe tomatoes can experience flavor reduction when refrigerated, but a day or two at room temperature before consumption may help restore some enzyme activity.

Thorough research, including taste testing, suggests that while fully ripe tomatoes gain minimal advantage from warmth, refrigeration causes minimal damage once they have reached ripeness. Storing tomatoes in a cool location with temperatures between 55°F 55°F (13°C) and 70°F (21°C), such as a wine cellar, can maintain freshness for a day or two without jeopardizing flavor.

For unripe tomatoes, avoid refrigeration. Keep them at room temperature, stem side down, away from direct sunlight. Cover the stem scar with tape to protect delicate shoulders if storing upside-down concerns you. Extremely unripe tomatoes can be placed in a paper bag to ripen in a cool environment.

Sliced tomatoes can be stored by tightly covering the cut side with plastic wrap, placing the tomato cut side down on a plate, and refrigerating it. For complete tomato slices, use a sealed food storage container or plastic bag and consume within three days.

If tomatoes are unripe, leave them on the kitchen counter until maturity. Once fully ripe, consume promptly or refrigerate to maintain freshness for up to two weeks.

While refrigeration is an option, it's crucial to consider ripeness. Refrigerating unripe tomatoes halts their development, and refrigerating excessively ripe tomatoes helps decelerate spoilage. However, regardless of the storage choice, allow tomatoes to return to room temperature before consumption for the most exquisite flavor.

Freezing tomatoes is also an option. Rinse, air-dry, remove stems, and freeze them in a suitable container. When ready to use, thaw in lukewarm water and peel off the skins. Frozen tomatoes are ideal for cooked dishes, while fresh tomatoes are best for dishes like salads or sandwiches.

In summary, store fully mature tomatoes at room temperature or in a cool location, avoid refrigerating unripe tomatoes and consider refrigeration for excessively ripe ones. Freezing is an option for preserving tomatoes, but each method contributes to different culinary experiences. Ultimately, whether fresh, refrigerated, or frozen, allowing tomatoes to reach room temperature before consumption ensures the most enjoyable flavor.

PRESERVING TOMATOES FOR THE LONG RUN

You can keep your tomatoes fresh for more than a week by choosing the right type. Go for varieties like Long Keeper Winter Storage tomatoes. If they're green, that's perfect – they'll ripen as they hang out. Store them in a cool, dark place, like a basement or closet, shielded from direct sunlight.

thought bubble: It is as if you are putting them in veggie witness protection – they're undercover, avoiding the spotlight until they're ripe and ready to reveal their true tomato identity. It's the secret agent mission of the produce drawer!

Check them weekly for any signs of mold or decay. If one goes bad, it can affect the others, so be vigilant!

For a different twist, you can dry your tomatoes. Wash them, cut them in half, and remove the seeds and stems. Place them on a dehydrator tray or a baking sheet in the oven. Let them dry at around 135°F (57°C) for about

4 hours, rotating them occasionally. Once they're leathery, not too crispy, they're done. You can preserve them in oil or freeze them for up to a year.

Cleaning is the first step here. Rinse your tomatoes and slice off the stem scar. Cut them into quarters or halves if you want smaller portions later. Arrange them on a plate or tray, freeze until solid, and then store them in a sealed container in the freezer for up to a year. If you prefer, you can easily peel off the skins after freezing.

Canning might sound a bit fancy, but it's worth it. Start by cleansing and blanching your tomatoes to get rid of the skins. Peel, remove seeds and excess juice and squeeze the pulp. Heat the tomatoes and liquid, add herbs if you like, then sanitize your canning jars. Transfer the tomatoes, remove bubbles, and seal the jars. Process them with a pressure canner, and you're good for up to a year.

If you're into crushed tomatoes, the process is quite similar. Clean and skin the tomatoes, quarter them, crush them with a wooden spoon, heat, and stir until they boil. Fill your jars, add lemon juice and salt, then can them for 35 to 45 minutes, depending on the jar size.

If you don't want to add extra liquid, that's fine, too. Clean and peel the tomatoes, load the jars, add lemon juice and salt, and process for 85 minutes in a boiling water canner.

For a head start on pasta sauce or soup, clean, peel, and dice your tomatoes. Cook them with celery, onion, green bell pepper, sugar, and salt. Spoon the stewed tomatoes into jars, process them in a pressure canner, and you're set!

Here's a recipe for homemade canned spaghetti sauce:

Ingredients:

- 10 lbs (about 4.5 kg) ripe tomatoes, peeled and diced

- 2 large onions, finely chopped

- 6 cloves garlic, minced

- 1/4 cup olive oil

- 2 teaspoons dried oregano

- 2 teaspoons dried basil

- 1 teaspoon dried thyme

- 1 teaspoon dried rosemary

- 1 teaspoon dried marjoram

- 1 teaspoon sugar

- 1 teaspoon salt (adjust to taste)

- 1/2 teaspoon black pepper

- 1/2 cup red wine (optional)

- 2 tablespoons tomato paste (optional, for added thickness)

- Lemon juice (for acidity, if necessary)

Instructions:

1. **Prepare Tomatoes:** Briefly blanch the tomatoes in boiling water for around 1 minute, then transfer them to an ice bath. Peel and dice the tomatoes, removing the seeds if preferred.

2. **Cook Onions and Garlic:** Heat olive oil in a large pot over medium heat. Add chopped onions and cook until soft and translucent. Introduce minced garlic and cook for an additional minute.

3. **Add Tomatoes:** Incorporate the diced tomatoes into the pot, ensuring a thorough mix with the onions and garlic.

4. **Season:** Stir in the dried oregano, basil, thyme, rosemary, marjoram, sugar, salt, and black pepper. If using red wine, add it now. Optionally, include tomato paste for additional thickness.

5. **Simmer:** Bring the mixture to a simmer, then reduce heat to low. Let it simmer uncovered for 2-3 hours, stirring occasionally. The

sauce should thicken, and the flavors should meld.

6. **Adjust Consistency and Seasoning:** If the sauce is too thin, continue simmering until it reaches the desired thickness. Taste and adjust the seasoning as necessary. Counteract acidity with a little sugar or add a splash of lemon juice for more acidity.

7. **Sterilize Jars:** While the sauce is cooking, sterilize your canning jars and lids by boiling them in hot water for about 10 minutes.

8. **Fill Jars:** Once the sauce is ready, carefully ladle it into the sterilized jars, leaving approximately 1/2 inch of headspace.

9. **Seal Jars:** Wipe the jar rims to ensure cleanliness, then place the sterilized lids on top. Screw on the metal bands until fingertip-tight.

10. **Process in a Water Bath (Optional):** To extend the sauce's shelf life, process the jars in a boiling water bath for about 35-40 minutes.

11. **Cool and Store:** Allow the jars to cool to room temperature, ensuring the lids have sealed properly. Store the sealed jars in a cool, dark place.

Now you have homemade canned spaghetti sauce ready whenever you crave a delicious pasta dish!

You can download a free pdf of "21 diverse recipes from various cuisines worldwide that use TOMATOES in their ingredients"

https://bit.ly/43hUFt6

We have briefly seen how tomatoes can be grown indoors and outdoors, but what if you don't have the ideal conditions for growing tomatoes? In the coming chapter, we will look at how tomatoes can be grown in extreme climates with just an extra bit of care.

Chapter Eight

You Can Grow Tomatoes Anywhere

D id you know that the temperature of the soil undergoes seasonal and daily fluctuations, driven by changes in radiant energy and energy transfers occurring at the soil surface. This temperature variation regulates the physical, chemical, and biological activities within the soil, influencing the exchange of gasses between the atmosphere and the soil.

But do you know what causes these fluctuations?

Environmental factors impact soil temperature by managing the heat input to the soil surface and the heat dissipation throughout the soil profile. Soil temperature impacts the decomposition rate of organic matter and the mineralization of diverse organic materials. Additionally, it has repercussions on soil water content, conductivity, and accessibility to plants.

Besides, elevated levels of humidity adversely affect plants by impeding the flow of air, impacting their capacity to "breathe" through stomata on the lower side of leaves.

When humidity becomes excessive, stomata close to minimize water loss, hindering the exchange of carbon dioxide and oxygen.

thought bubble: *It's like the stomata are the overzealous security guards of the plant, shutting down the CO2 and O2 exchange faster than a senior's door curfew!*

This closure, combined with saturated leaves, establishes an environment where plants encounter difficulties in transpiring efficiently. Extended periods of heightened humidity result in an incapacity to evaporate water or extract nutrients from the soil, leading to decay. Conversely, low humidity in warm settings amplifies transpiration rates, demanding heightened fertilization.

Efficient control of the climate becomes vital, averting challenges such as the proliferation of mold, root decay, and infestations by pests associated with humid conditions.

So, how can you overcome these challenges and protect your tomatoes from the adverse effects of climate?

Let's learn.

How Plant Container Material Impacts Health

If you prefer growing tomatoes in a container, familiarizing yourself with the containers best for planting tomatoes can be helpful for you.

There are different types of containers appropriate for cultivating tomatoes on your patio or deck, and these containers vary in form and dimensions.

An ideal container must possess sufficient size to accommodate ample soil and roots.

Most container gardeners typically opt for more sizable containers (5 gallons or above), modest to intermediate size (1 to 3 gallons), or suspended baskets.

Choosing a container that is insufficient in size for the specific tomato type can be a huge mistake.

Tomatoes have a huge root system, and when confined, they yield a diminished quantity of fruits.

Which is something you might not want.

Even tomato varieties recommended for thriving in 1 or 2-gallon containers will probably exhibit superior performance in bigger pots. When uncertain, opt for a larger container rather than a smaller one.

Speaking of containers to grow tomatoes there are different materials these containers are made up of.

Terra cotta and clay are organic options for tomatoes, seamlessly harmonizing with various surroundings.

Natural materials also facilitate effective ventilation, allowing air and water to circulate efficiently. However, remember that terra cotta and unglazed pottery tend to dehydrate rapidly, necessitating frequent monitoring to ensure tomatoes receive adequate water.

Additionally, abrupt temperature fluctuations can render pottery more susceptible to cracking compared to alternative materials. There may be a need for more frequent replacement of clay pots than containers crafted from different substances.

Functional and cost-effective, plastic vessels have emerged as a highly favored choice for containers. They endure freeze-thaw cycles effectively. Plastic also readily retains moisture – the soil in plastic pots typically demands less frequent watering.

Another common material planting containers are made up of is wood. Redwood, cedar, and cypress are the most resistant to decay among the woods employed in container construction. Steer clear of pressure-treated wood due to its chemicals leaching into the soil. Wood offers superb insulation. On the flip side, wooden containers might incur a higher cost than their plastic counterparts.

Container materials such as concrete, fiberglass, cast iron, wire, compressed paper, metal, and even recycled items like old buckets, wheelbarrows, and garbage cans are all viable for cultivating tomatoes in containers. Gardeners establish drainage holes in the bottom using a hammer and a large nail. Some individuals even cultivate tomatoes in black plastic refuse bags.

Ensure your chosen container offers sufficient space for root system development and features punched drainage holes at the base.

thought bubble: *Make sure your plant's home is not the horticultural version of a cramped apartment without windows – we want happy roots, not leafy complaints about the lack of space!*

When Temperatures and Humidity Sore

Intense summer temperatures can halt the productivity of your once-thriving tomato plants. When temperatures reach 85°F to 90°F (30°C to 32°C) during the day and stay above 75°F (24°C) at night, the pollination of tomato flowers frequently falters, leading to their subsequent drop — consequently hindering the production of new fruit. The prolonged duration of high temperatures extends the pause in tomato flower activity. In short, warm weather has the potential to defer your tomato crop. (Reid-StJohn, 2014)

Tomato varieties resistant to high temperatures, such as Heatmaster, Solar Fire, Summer Set, and Phoenix, can develop fruit even in rising temperatures. These tomatoes are often labeled as "heat set" varieties, featuring heat-related terms or locations in their names. Alternatively, following the approach of professional tomato cultivators, consider planting determinate types that tend to ripen their fruit in a concentrated period earlier in the growing season—before the intense heat sets in.

But if you live in an area with a hot climate, here are three important measures that you can take to keep your plants safe from the adverse effects of humidity and high temperatures.

Planting in the right place

Tomatoes require ample sunlight, ideal for regions like the Midwest, Northeast, or Pacific Northwest. However, in Southern California, the Deep South, Texas, and the Desert Southwest, where summer afternoons can reach scorching temperatures, consider selecting locations where tomatoes can bask in morning sunlight, followed by filtered sun or gentle shade for the remainder of the day. In places lacking natural shade, craft some shade on your own. Additionally, ensure you're planting in fertile, nutrient-rich soil.

Shade

You can employ shade fabric to cool tomatoes during the crucial hours when tomato flower pollination usually takes place (typically between 10 am and 2 pm).

Studies indicate that optimal yields are achieved with a shade structure open to the east (no fabric on that side), allowing the plants to bask in morning sunlight while being shielded from the intense afternoon rays.

To construct your own shade, fashion a frame around tomatoes using wood or row cover hoops, then cover it with shade fabric.

Look for "50 percent" shade fabric, reducing sunlight by 50 percent and heat by 25 percent. Alternatively, experiment with lightweight row covers for summer, typically providing around 15 percent shade. In regions with less intense sunlight and heat, shading tomatoes is generally unnecessary.

Mulch

Apply a mulch layer, approximately 2 to 3 inches thick, around tomato plants to assist in retaining soil moisture. In areas with extended growing periods, renew the mulch as it decomposes (consider late summer). Opt for organic substances such as straw, cotton hulls, shredded bark, chopped leaves, untreated grass clippings, or other materials locally accessible, as they enhance the soil while breaking down.

GROWING TOMATOES IN HOT, DRY CONDITIONS

Although tomatoes thrive in hot, humid conditions, hot and dry climates are a different story and the soil can quickly cause plants to wilt and drop blossoms (flowers that fall off before the fruit appears).

thought bubble: Tomatoes in hot, dry climates are like the drama queens of the garden. They'll wilt faster than a leaf in a Shakespearean tragedy if the soil isn't to their liking.

A 2-inch layer of compost, grass clippings, or manure can help retain moisture but peat moss can hold up to 20 times its weight in water. Remove lower leaves from seedlings as this will encourage more root growth to absorb moisture. Plant tomatoes with cages rather than stakes. There will be less need for pruning and the fruit will be better protected from direct sunlight. (Mentors, 2022b)

Here is a list of some tomato varieties that can do well in hot climate:

Beefmaster tomato
Celebrity tomato
Early girl tomato
Sweet hundred tomato
Arkansas Traveler tomato
Brandywine OTV tomato
Burbank slicing tomato
Costoluto Genovese tomato
Eva Purple Ball tomato
Great White Beefsteak
Marvel Stiped tomato
Purple Calabash tomato
Thessaloniki tomato
Yellow Pear tomato (Tomatoes for
Hot Dry Climates, n.d.)

SPECIAL CARE FOR COLDER WEATHER

Like hot and humid climate can affect your tomatoes, cold weather has its effects too.

However, even when cultivating tomatoes in chilly, damp conditions, it's still possible to yield excellent fruit. Achieving this may necessitate additional cautious gardening techniques.

First step involves research. Do a thorough research of the tomato varieties that do well in your area and choose the ones that are suitable according to the climatic conditions you have.

Here's a list of varieties that can be grown in cold weather:

Celebrity tomato
Golden Nugget tomato
Husky Gold tomato
Orange Pixie tomato
Oregon Spring tomato
Siltez Tomato
Bush beefsteak tomato
Galian's tomato
Glacier tomato
Gregori's Altai tomato
Grushovka tomato
Kimberly tomato
Legend tomato
Manitoba tomato
New Yorker tomato

Polar Baby tomato (Best Tomatoes for
Cold Climates, n.d.)

Successfully growing tomatoes in cold, wet weather demands strategic gardening practices, especially when dealing with challenging climates.

First of all, protecting tomatoes from rain is significantly important in cooler climates, as damp conditions can invite blight. Green houses or hoop houses can offer a practical solution. These structures trap heat, shielding plants from rain while allowing essential airflow.

thought bubble: *Shielding tomatoes from rain is a must; otherwise, they act like they're auditioning for the Olympics synchronized swimming team – a tomato water ballet extravaganza you didn't sign up for!*

Be cautious not to overheat the plants on sunny days and ensure proper watering of the roots, avoiding splashing on top growth.

The timeline for successful tomato cultivation in cold, wet weather spans from February to November. You can start with indoor seed sowing, progressing to transplanting and hardening off in April and May. By June, you can transplant the tomatoes to a sunny location, shielded from rainfall with hoop houses. In July, meticulous management involves opening tunnels on hot days and closing them during cold, wet spells. August brings continued care and potential pruning, while September and October demand additional measures like tipping out plants and removing late flowers. (Mentors, 2022).

While you put in the effort to keep your plants healthy in the winter, do not forget that they need a certain amount of sunlight. Colder regions might lack sufficient light. Therefore, you can grow lights for your tomatoes.

Employing LED grow lights for winter tomato cultivation offers substantial benefits. These lights contribute to enhanced yields and quality by providing a tailored spectrum of red and blue LEDs, expediting ripening and ensuring a balanced plant structure.

LED lights generate the right amount of heat, preventing damage to the crops, and can be actively water-cooled, maintaining a stable growing climate. With the ability to control light intensity, you can optimize conditions for tomatoes, fostering vitality, stress resistance, and disease resilience. Overall, the use of LED grow lights proves advantageous in sustaining healthy and productive tomato crops during the winter season. (Keating, 2023)

Grow lights may also be necessary in a greenhouse. On that note, some people in extremely cold climates may need a greenhouse but they might not be at the stage of building a full-sized greenhouse as a beginner.

However, they can create a DIY greenhouse.

Creating your own DIY greenhouse can be a rewarding project that adds functionality and aesthetic appeal to your space. Here are a few ideas that you can use.

• Repurpose old windows by screwing them together to create a protective space for seedlings. Add a hinged door and decorative metal corbels for a gabled roof frame.

• Convert an old curio cabinet into a greenhouse by cleaning it thoroughly and adding grow lights to each shelf. Manage optimal growing conditions by scheduling the lights with outlet timers.

• Enhance a store-bought mini greenhouse with a sage green paint coat and terra-cotta roof tiles. This simple upgrade transforms the greenhouse into a custom-looking structure with minimal effort.

• Use a decorative lantern designed for candles as a mini greenhouse. The glass provides warmth, and adding a small grow light can further improve the plant environment.

• Plant outdoor pots early by inserting translucent umbrellas to protect delicate plants from cool nighttime temperatures. This simple solution creates instant mini greenhouses tailored to each pot. (Young, 2022)

You can go ahead and go creative with designing your DIY greenhouse. Doing so is one of the ways to get healthier plants. Another innovative way is to employ a hydroponic system.

Tomato Varieties for Hydroponics Systems

A hydroponic system is a method of growing plants without soil, using a nutrient-rich water solution to deliver essential minerals directly to the plant roots. This innovative approach allows precise control over environmental factors, such as pH, nutrient levels, and temperature. Hydroponics can be implemented through various systems, including Deep Water Culture (DWC), Nutrient Film Technique (NFT), and Aeroponics, each offering distinct advantages for plant growth.

thought bubble: *Hydroponics is like the plant version of a five-star spa – no soil, just a nutrient-rich water bath. It's the treatment they deserve, where they get pampered with a customized menu of nutrients and a spa day without the mess of mud masks!*

Hydroponic systems offer numerous advantages, including year-round cultivation, higher crop yields, and the ability to grow in controlled indoor environments. By providing direct access to nutrients, plants in hydroponic systems often exhibit faster growth rates and increased nutrient absorption. Additionally, these systems reduce the need for pesticides, resulting in cleaner and healthier produce. Hydroponics also allows for space-efficient farming, making it suitable for urban environments.

If that sounds interesting, you can establish a hydroponic system too.

To do so, begin by selecting the right type of hydroponic method based on factors like space, resources, and budget. Common systems include Deep Water Culture (DWC), Nutrient Film Technique (NFT), and Aeroponics.

Once you have chosen, set up the system by assembling the necessary components and ensuring a suitable location with adequate light and temperature control. Select a nutrient-rich medium like Coco Coir or Perlite for seedling germination. Monitor and maintain crucial factors such as pH, temperature, nutrient levels, and light to ensure optimal plant growth and a healthy hydroponic crop. (Prasanniya, 2023)

And with this, you've completed this chapter. Regardless of where you are in the world, it's easy to see how temperatures and the weather are changing, not just on the odd day but for weeks and months on end. It's always a good idea to have a backup plan and know what options are available in case you notice your climate is starting to change and your usual tomato care isn't enough.

Even with extensive information, we may run into issues when growing tomatoes. In the final chapter, we will cover some common problems you may encounter on your tomato adventure and how to overcome them.

Chapter Nine

Overcoming Troubles with Your Tomatoes

"The tomato hides its grief. Internal damage is hard to spot." – Julia Child

In this chapter, we will delve into the intricate balance of cultivating robust tomato plants by prioritizing prevention over cure. A brief overview of potential diseases and pests will be provided, but our primary focus will revolve around understanding and mitigating environmental stressors.

So, without any further ado, let's get started.

Blossom Drop

thought bubble: *It feels awesome to see a few things drop. For example, beats in a catchy song, jaw's at a magic show and even your best friend's smartphone when standing by a lake. But trust me blossom drop is that one thing you wouldn't like to see. It's like seeing all your efforts going down the drain before your eyes.*

Tomato blossom drop is a frustrating issue for home gardeners, where healthy-looking tomato plants develop blossoms that eventually dry up and fall off before fruit formation. Common causes include extreme temperatures, insufficient pollination, nitrogen imbalance, humidity extremes, water scarcity, insect damage, and excessively heavy fruit.

The primary culprit is often temperature stress, with daytime highs above 85°F (29°C), nighttime highs above 70°F (21°C), or low nighttime temperatures below 55°F (13°C) triggering blossom drop.

Preventative measures involve selecting climate-suited tomato varieties, ensuring proper pollination, controlling fertilizer use, managing humidity, deep watering, and maintaining overall plant health to minimize stress and optimize fruit set. (Iannotti, 2021)

Cracked Fruit

Tomato fruit cracking, a frequent issue in coastal South (US) regions, results from abrupt changes in soil moisture, particularly after dry spells. Intense rainfall, typical in this locale, triggers swift fruit expansion, surpassing the tomato skin's growth capacity. There are two common damage patterns: radial cracking along the fruit's sides in hot, humid conditions, and concentric cracking circling the stem end.

A cracked tomato is a sad sight to behold

To avert this, maintaining steady soil moisture with appropriate watering, employing soaker hoses, drip irrigation, and mulching becomes pivotal. A prompt harvest of cracked fruits is recommended to prevent rot, ensuring superior flavor in ripening tomatoes. (Glen, n.d.)

Sunscald

Sunscald affects tomatoes and peppers exposed to direct sunlight in high temperatures, especially on plants with minimal foliage or previous leaf loss from disease. It's common on areas once shaded but suddenly exposed, causing white or yellow blisters on green fruit.

141

Prolonged exposure can result in papery, flattened, grayish-white patches prone to mold and rot. To prevent this, ensure plants are healthy with ample foliage, practice regular watering, opt for low nitrogen fertilizers, and use mulch.

Shelter exposed fruit with shade cloth, choose disease-resistant varieties, and consider organic methods like appropriate fertilizers for added protection. (Sunscald of Tomato and Peppers, n.d.)

Poor Quality Fruit

thought bubble: *"Patience is bitter, but its fruit is sweet."*
If only there weren't a lot of hidden conditions attached to this statement, the life of a gardener would be very easy. The truth is a lot can go wrong if one is not careful enough.

The emergence of subpar tomato fruits, characterized by stunted growth or deformities, stems from diverse challenges in the cultivation process. Common triggers encompass insufficient pollination, nutrient scarcities—particularly in potassium and phosphorus—excessive nitrogen, erratic watering, tomato ailments like late blight, insufficient sunlight, and extreme weather conditions.

Safeguarding measures involve fostering a thriving garden ecosystem with ample pollinators, ensuring a well-rounded nutritional profile, steering clear of nitrogen excess, maintaining steady moisture levels, averting diseases through meticulous soil management, optimizing sunlight exposure, and shielding plants from severe weather. Adherence to these methods heightens the probability of a resilient, high-quality tomato yield. (Hailey, 2023)

Catfacing

Catfacing, a physiological anomaly in tomatoes, results from irregular development of flower buds, leading to enlarged or perforated blossom scars. This condition, not entirely comprehended, heightens the vulnerability of fruit to black mold rot in specific environmental circumstances.

Contributors to catfacing encompass cold temperatures during flowering, temperature fluctuations, excessive pruning, elevated nitrogen levels, and thrip-induced damage to flower pistils.

It doesn't look much like cat's face

To avert catfacing, avoid excessive pruning and nitrogen fertilization, uphold appropriate greenhouse temperatures, opt for catfacing-resistant varieties, and carefully time any high tunnel planting. These measures diminish the likelihood of distorted tomato fruits arising from catfacing. (Anonymous, 2019)

Leaf Curling

thought bubble: *There are many things that look awesome when curled such as ribbons on birthday presents, ancient scrolls, and even a cat's tail during a cozy nap. But one thing you'd never want to see curled is your tomato leaves; they're not aiming for the "garden fashion" trend. There's something horrible going on in there.*

Tomato leaf curling, a prevalent problem for gardeners, stems from diverse factors with effective precautionary measures. Elevated temperatures surpassing 90°F (32°C), strong sunlight exposure, and inadequate watering are primary triggers, compelling the plant to retain water through leaf curling.

Insufficient soil nutrition, particularly surplus nitrogen or inadequacies in potassium and phosphorus, plays a role in curled leaves. Furthermore, viral infections such as yellow leaf curl virus and herbicide drift can induce this phenomenon.

To combat leaf curling, explore shading methods, correct watering routines, soil enhancements, routine soil analysis, and attentive plant maintenance, reducing the impact of environmental stressors on tomato plants. (Hutchinson, 2022)

Puffy Tomatoes

Inflated tomatoes, distinguished by void interiors, arise from insufficient pollination during flowering or complications in early seed development. Elements like inappropriate temperatures, abundant rainfall impacting pollination, and imbalances in nitrogen and potassium levels during fertilization contribute to this phenomenon, recognized as puffiness in tomatoes. Although existing hollow fruits cannot be rectified, forestalling future incidents entails executing a soil examination before fertilizing to ensure proper nutrient levels.

Specific tomato varieties intentionally crafted to possess hollowness must not be mistaken for those affected by puffiness. Appropriate spacing, meticulous pruning, and curbing nitrogen fertilizer use aid in averting severe issues such as bacterial stem rot in tomato plants. (Waterworth, 2021)

And with this, you have completed the final chapter of this book.

They say you have to fall off a horse 7 times before you can call yourself a rider. Gardening is a little similar. If everything went perfectly well all the time, you wouldn't really learn anything. Anything less than a perfect harvest of tomatoes can be disheartening, but it is an opportunity to make slight adjustments and grow an even better yield of tomatoes.

So, my fellow tomato lovers, let's buckle our shoes and start working to achieve our dream tomato garden.

Chapter Ten

How to Protect Tomato Plants from Pests and Diseases

T he very first thing that pops in our mind is pesticide when it comes to preventing plants from pests and diseases. But using pesticides has a number of drawbacks.

thought bubble: *Think of pesticides as the meddling villains in your tomatoes' love story with you – they might promise a quick fix, but they bring a host of unwanted drama to the garden plot. Let's keep the romance alive with healthier, eco-friendly alternatives!*

Luckily there is an entire list of organic solutions to this problem. You can choose from them.

Whatever you do, don't reach for that pesticide! It will contaminate soil and water but worse than that, it will kill all of the wonderful, beneficial insects we need. Tomato hornworms can devour a plant in a matter of days but parasitic wasps eat hornworms. A pesticide isn't going to differentiate between a hornworm and a parasitic wasp, it's just going to kill everything.

You need to be vigilant and protect your tomatoes from these pests that can destroy your garden.

Pests that Love Tomatoes

Pests are the villain in your garden. They not only assail your flora but can also transmit diseases themselves. To put it differently, if you haven't yet, you ought to emphasize pest management in your tomato garden.

These ten prevalent tomato pests are the most troublesome ones to be vigilant about.

1: Aphids

These creatures possess pliable pear-shaped forms and usually appear in shades of white, black, brown, or occasionally pink.

They reside on fresh stems and the lower surface of juvenile foliage. These are juice-extracting bugs that leave a viscous residue, luring a diverse array of other bothersome insects.

thought bubble: *Think of Aphids as Count Dracula. Only you can save your garden from turning into Hotel Transylvania.*

You can readily eliminate them by wiping or plucking with your fingers. Alternatively, use a water spray bottle to wash them away from the tomato plant without causing harm. Another prevalent solution involves applying a natural soap blend with a spray bottle to smother the insects.

In severe instances, trimming or squeezing impacted leaves or other plant sections might become essential.

2: Cutworms

Cutworms have the potential to devastate a tomato plant within a single night. These caterpillars, appearing in shades of gray or brown with black or yellow markings, measure around two inches in length and cause considerable harm.

These covert larvae do their damage during the night, creating sizable gaps in your tomatoes. However, it's not only the fruit that suffers. Seedlings usually bear the brunt of their impact, but cutworms also assault the stems, leading to the eventual collapse of the plant. In daylight hours, they conceal themselves beneath the soil or amidst plant remnants.

To thwart cutworm infestations, regularly cultivate the soil and eliminate any remnants of plant matter before planting tomatoes. Additionally, placing collars around the stem base is recognized as an effective means to discourage the worms. The moment you identify a cutworm, merely pluck them off using your hands.

3. Flea beetles

These petite leaping insects are glossy dark brown or black beetles, reminiscent of fleas, sometimes with white or yellow stripes.

thought bubble: *Don't be fooled by their beauty, they are a curse in disguise!*

Adult beetles reach a mere one-tenth of an inch in size. Sprouting seeds face the greatest susceptibility to flea beetles, and these bugs frequently harbor numerous bacterial and viral illnesses that can harm plant well-being.

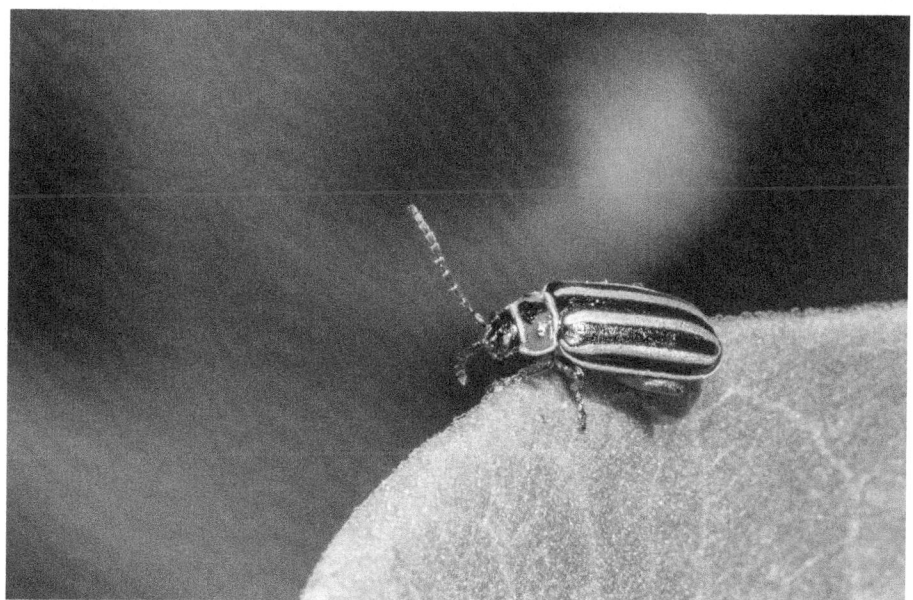

Similar to addressing cutworms, practice crop rotation, clear away debris, and cultivate your soil.

To manage infestations, you can sprinkle diatomaceous soil on your plants. This substance is employed to deter and manage various other pest infestations on tomato plants and other flora in your garden.

Several effective methods can deter flea beetles from establishing in your soil and leaves, such as employing row covers and setting up yellow adhesive traps to ensnare adult beetles.

4. Root-Knot Nematodes

Various nematode species exist, with some even serving as agents to manage detrimental pests. Nevertheless, root-knot nematodes fall into the category of harmful insects.

These minuscule worms induce wilting, yellowing of leaves, and stunted growth in plants. Additionally, in alignment with their name, they prompt the enlargement of tomato roots, forming knob-like growths. Root-knot nematodes are prevalent in regions with warm climates and brief winters.

Managing these pests proves challenging. They frequently catch a lift on gardening equipment and footwear, emphasizing the essential need for proper gardening cleanliness.

Maintaining the rotation of crops remains crucial. Nematodes require multiple seasons to integrate into the soil. Employing crop rotation and cultivating the soil will hinder their establishment.

Choosing nematode-resistant tomatoes serves as an ideal natural preventive step. Look for varieties with an "N" designation next to their names.

5. Blister Beetles

Blister beetles exhibit a substantial appetite for tomato foliage and, when neglected, can entirely strip your plant of its leaves. Despite their harm to tomato plants and others, they are most renowned for their impact on humans. When crushed or injured, they emit the blistering substance, cantharidin.

Blister beetles display hues of black, red, or gray with striped patterns. They are prevalent in the Midwest, as well as the eastern and southern regions of the United States.

Effectively managing this pest involves removing them with protected hands and promptly eliminating affected plants. When plucking them off, deposit the beetles into a compact container filled with soapy water to hinder their flight.

In case large groups of blister beetles pose a concern in your area, shield your tomato plants with securely positioned row covers.

6. Hornworm

Another detrimental caterpillar variety is the hornworm. These insects surpass the typical size, reaching approximately three inches in length. Their light green hue allows them to seamlessly camouflage with tomato and other plant leaves, rendering them challenging to detect and eliminate. Tomato hornworms, in particular, feature a distinct straight black horn, simplifying identification upon sighting.

They have the capability to strip the leaves from an entire plant and, although extremely infrequently, might assault the exterior of tomato fruits. Additionally, they deposit eggs on the lower surfaces of the leaves.

thought bubble: They prepare an entire army of hornworms to attack your garden. Stop them before they conquer your tomato plants one by one!

Given their dimensions, manually plucking them off is the simplest solution.

7. Slugs and Snails

Slugs and snails are prevalent inhabitants of gardens. Despite their seemingly harmless and endearing appearance, their feeding patterns can cause significant harm to tomato plants. They leave conspicuous gaps in both leaves and fruit, accompanied by a path of mucous. Thriving in damp settings, they exhibit heightened activity during the night, rendering them challenging to identify.

Effective management revolves around regulating their population. Optimal methods to deter slugs and snails from tomatoes involve manually removing them, adjusting watering routines, or employing a beer trap.

For a beer trap, fill a container or pail with beer and position it at ground level in the garden near the plants. The beer entices the slugs and will perish upon landing in it. Watering in the morning consistently ensures that the upper soil layer and leaves dry up by evening.

8. Spider Mites

thought bubble: *Spider mites are a polar opposite of what you'll find in Spider Man. The latter is the savior and the former is the destroyer. The latter won't visit your garden (well, unless you live in the movie) and the former won't leave your garden once they make an appearance.*

They are widespread in diverse climates but tend to thrive in warm and arid conditions. They congregate in sizable clusters, taking residence on the lower side of leaves. The delicate webbing encircling leaves and stems serve as a revealing sign of their presence.

A prevalent indication of spider mites is the yellowing or reddish hue of leaves. These diminutive arachnids extract the sap from the plant, ultimately leading to defoliation as impacted leaves persistently wither and drop.

Despite their small size, they exhibit notable resistance to numerous insect sprays, and their substantial population proves challenging to regulate. Nevertheless, the strategy lies in overseeing their surroundings. Consistent and proper watering aids in diminishing spider mites, as does the introduction of beneficial parasitic pests. Oil-based sprays also prove effective in addressing minor infestations.

Nevertheless, if the intricate webbing persists in constricting the tomato plant and its condition continues to decline, you might have to eliminate the plant to curb further dissemination.

9. Tomato Fruit Worms

Tomato fruit worms, alternatively referred to as corn earworms, rank as one of the most destructive pests for tomatoes. They are notorious for inflicting damage on tomatoes, peppers, corn, and even tobacco.

These larvae consume tomato leaves and pulp, resulting in deformed leaves. Their young bore into the stems and fruits, making them exceptionally challenging to detect and extract without causing harm to the plant.

Grown tomato fruit worms manifest as moths. Their larvae exhibit a greyish-yellow hue and measure approximately two inches in length, laid within white eggs. These eggs are situated on the underside of smaller leaves, in proximity to the fruits. Upon hatching, the larvae tunnel into nearby fruit.

thought bubble: *It's crucial to protect your garden in this critical condition. Put on your Sherlock-Holmes-hat and let's get to the business.*

Manually remove the worms or eggs promptly upon detection. An effective natural choice to eliminate tomato fruit worms involves introducing natural adversaries, such as minute pirate bugs and specific varieties of wasps. Steer clear of planting tomatoes in close proximity to corn and entirely eradicate all contaminated fruit once recognized.

10. Whitefly

Whiteflies are diminutive insects, akin to aphids, predominantly impacting tomatoes cultivated in greenhouses or indoor settings. Similar to aphids, these nuisances thrive on extracting sap from the plant, influencing the overall development of your vegetation. The consequence is yellowing leaves and diminished yield.

Swift prevention and management of whitefly infestations are crucial, given their potential to transmit diseases. Beneficial insects like ladybugs can effectively diminish whitefly populations. Additionally, horticultural oil proves useful in smothering whiteflies at any life stage.

Cultivating the soil, changing crop positions, employing proper watering techniques, maintaining overall plant well-being, and vigilantly watching for indications of pests are indispensable instruments in preventing pest issues. As an added benefit, they will also shield your plants from diseases.

DISEASES TO WATCH OUT FOR

Maintaining a thriving yield of tomatoes involves vigilant monitoring for ailments triggered by fungi, bacteria, and viruses, leading to leaf blemishes and blights. Challenges may also arise from temperature fluctuations, nutrient imbalances, and moisture variations, jeopardizing your harvest and the prospect of relishing homegrown tomato slices in your upcoming BLT.

Mitigate these potential issues by acquainting yourself with their indicators and implementing a handful of simple tactics.

Opting for varieties resistant to diseases, ensuring adequate plant spacing, applying mulch, and providing a minimum of 1 inch of weekly watering are crucial measures to maintain the health of your tomato plants. Numerous prevalent plant ailments and pests hide in the soil, underscoring the importance of regularly changing the location of your tomato planting to avoid reusing the same ground within a four-year span. Diseases can also propagate in moist conditions, emphasizing the need to refrain from clustering tomatoes closely. This promotes improved air circulation and accelerates leaf drying.

thought bubble: Besides, clustered plants can give shelter to diseases aiding them to execute on their mischievous plans, propagate in your garden and destroy it.

Direct your watering efforts towards the root base of your tomato plants to reduce splashing on the foliage. Additionally, irrigate in the morning, allowing ample time for the leaves to dry before the onset of cooler evening temperatures.

Tomatoes typically exhibit robust growth and yield abundantly when cultivated in abundant sunlight with ample water and nutrients. However, it's nearly unavoidable that these plants will encounter leaf diseases or flawed fruit.

Following are the most common tomato plant diseases:

Septoria Leaf Spot

Septoria leaf spot is triggered by a fungus, manifesting as petite, circular patches featuring a center that appears grayish-white and edges that are dark. Each blemish may exhibit minuscule black spots at its core. Leaves affected by this ailment take on a yellow hue, undergo wilting, and eventually drop off. This tomato plant disease thrives in extended periods of warm and damp conditions, with spores rapidly disseminating to other leaves through splashing water.

Refrain from irrigating tomatoes from above, as the mist may propel the spores evolving on the leaves back into the soil, perpetuating the cycle of the disease. Employ a spray designed to combat fungal diseases.

Anthracnose

thought bubble: *This fungus is another uninvited guest that doesn't require any passport or legal documentation to enter the territory of your garden. That's really unethical. I wish technology could teach plant diseases some morals.*

Anthracnose manifests as a diminutive, circular, depressed region on tomato fruits. Over time, concentric rings develop around the initial spot. The flesh of the fruit may undergo complete rotting, particularly in the case of overripe tomatoes, underscoring the importance of promptly harvesting fruits as they ripen. Spores propagate through water splashes, and the prevalence of this fungus is highest during periods of warm and damp weather.

Alter your watering techniques to ensure water drips onto the roots, avoiding contact with the leaves. Gather tomatoes when they are fully ripe, as excessively ripe ones are more susceptible to the fungus compared to tomatoes in the initial phases of ripening.

Fusarium and Verticillium Wilt

Wilt diseases stem from soil-inhabiting fungi that infiltrate via young roots, subsequently obstructing the vessels responsible for transporting water to the plant's roots and stems. Insufficient water leads to wilting during sunny days, though there may be apparent recovery during the night. Initially, tomato wilt might manifest in either the upper or lower leaves, resulting in discoloration and subsequent dieback from the tips. This progression persists until the entire plant succumbs to the affliction.

To manage these diseases affecting tomato plants, choose tomatoes specifically bred for resistance. Look for labels indicating resistance to verticillium (V), fusarium (F, FF, or FFF variations). If tomato wilt is encountered, refrain from utilizing the area for growing tomatoes, eggplants, potatoes, and peppers for 4 to 6 years. The fungi responsible for tomato wilt can persist in the soil for an extended period without a new host for infection.

Rest in peace, dear gardening plans!

When dealing with fusarium wilt, the most effective strategy is a proactive one. Rotate your crops to avoid planting tomatoes in the same garden area yearly. Opt for varieties resistant to wilting if you've experienced tomato losses due to wilting diseases previously, as the fungus has the potential to persist in both garden and lawn soils during winter.

When plants are afflicted, there's limited recourse for treating Verticillium wilt. Employ crop rotation, as the fungus can endure extended durations in the soil and coexist with weeds like ragweed. Opting for varieties resistant to wilt is the most effective means to thwart Verticillium wilt.

Early Blight (Alternaria)

An additional fungal affliction affecting tomato plants, Alternaria, triggers early blight. On lower leaves, distinctive brown or black spots emerge with dark borders, resembling a target pattern. Fruits' stem ends may also be affected, displaying sizable, depressed black regions with concentric rings. Typically, this fungus manifests after the plants have initiated fruit production.

Crop rotation prevents new plants from contracting the disease. Avoid planting tomatoes, eggplants or peppers in the same spot each year as these can all be infected with early blight. A garden fungicide can treat infected plants.

Late Blight

This rapidly spreading ailment in tomato plants stems from the fungus Phytophthora infestans, typically emerging in cool, rainy periods towards the conclusion of a growing season. Resembling frost damage, it manifests as irregular green-black patches on leaves. Fruits may exhibit sizable, irregularly shaped brown blemishes that swiftly deteriorate. Notably, this plant disease also impacts potatoes and can be transmitted from them.

Mosaic Virus

The mosaic virus, a prevalent ailment in tomato plants, afflicts various plant species. Although it doesn't result in plant fatality, it significantly reduces both the quantity and quality of fruits produced. Named for its distinct markings resembling a mosaic in light green and yellow on leaves, along with mottling on affected plant fruits, the virus also induces the growth of leaves in deformed shapes reminiscent of ferns.

Given that the virus infiltrates through lesions in leaves and stems, minimize direct contact with the plant. It also targets tobacco plants and can be conveyed from them if you've recently interacted with cigarettes or other tobacco items. If you smoke, ensure thorough handwashing with soap and wear gardening gloves when dealing with tomatoes.

After reviewing these issues with tomatoes and suspecting a viral disease, apply neem oil to your tomato plants. Effectively managing soil and utilizing organic fertilizer for tomatoes contributes to plant health, enhancing their innate ability to resist viruses.

Blossom Drop

Caused by drastic temperature fluctuations, blossom drop happens when temperatures exceed 85°F (29°C) or fall below 58°F (14°C). These extremes harm developing tomato blossoms, and the impact may go unnoticed until you have fewer tomatoes to gather later in the season. To avert blossom drop, employ row covers to elevate night temperatures. While mitigating hot daytime temperatures is challenging, focus on sustaining robust plants to encourage new bud development after the heatwave subsides.

Though you can't control the weather, bolster the overall plant vigor by applying tomato fertilizer, attracting pollinators by cultivating milkweed and cosmos, and utilizing neem oil insecticides.

Blossom-End Rot

Attributed to insufficient calcium, often due to varying water availability, blossom-end rot is a prevalent issue affecting tomatoes, specifically impacting the fruit. Manifesting as a depressed, lifeless region opposite the stem (at the blossom-end of the fruit), this area enlarges as the fruit matures. Mitigate blossom-end rot by fostering consistent, pressure-free plant development. Ensure regular watering to sustain adequately moist, yet not waterlogged, soil. Apply a 2-inch-deep coating of mulch around plants to preserve soil moisture.

Prior to planting tomatoes, arrange for your local garden store or Cooperative Extension to conduct a soil examination. They can provide guidance on adjusting your soil, with the addition of lime and gypsum for calcium, tailored to your soil's condition. Enhance calcium naturally by incorporating crushed eggshells into your compost when amending the soil. For mid-season prevention of blossom end rot on tomatoes, employ a foliar spray containing calcium chloride. Administer it early in the morning or late in the day, as spraying leaves in the midday can result in burns. Ensure uniform water application by watering plants consistently at the same time daily.

Damping Off

An aggravating fungal affliction affecting tomato plants, damping off leads to the abrupt failure of seedlings or an inability to germinate. Facilitate quicker germination by pre-soaking seeds, and refrain from planting them in chilly soil. When using potting mix for seed planting, consistently opt for a new bag and sterilize your containers beforehand with a 10% bleach solution (mixing one part bleach with nine parts water). Ensure the soil's top layer dries between watering sessions.

Sunscald

Similar to a sunburn on tomatoes, sunscald results in a portion of the fruit turning tender, paler, and desiccated. Ward off sunscald by preserving ample foliage to provide shade for fruits or by artificially shielding fruits using a shade cloth.

Utilizing tomato cages or a wire support structure enveloping the plants offers optimal branch reinforcement while naturally providing shade to developing tomatoes. Sunscald is more likely to happen on staked plants that have been excessively pruned, exposing numerous tomatoes to direct sunlight. Retaining some foliage and branches ensures shading during the most intense part of the day.

Organic Disease and Pest Control

Don't be deceived by the names early blight and late blight; these can manifest at any point in the year. Septoria leaf spot is recognized by petite, dark circular marks often surrounded by yellow halos, initially emerging on the lower leaves. Early blight can infiltrate stems and leaves, presenting lesions with concentric rings. Late blight impacts extensive leaf areas, exhibiting a white and fuzzy appearance on the leaf's underside, swiftly causing crop destruction. It's noteworthy that both early and late blight also affect potatoes, with late blight being the cause of the Irish potato famine.

These ailments can spread through various means, and understanding their nature can offer easy remedies. Adequate moisture, particularly on the leaves, creates favorable conditions for the spores of these diseases. Watering at the plant's base can mitigate this issue; if you opt for a sprinkler system or a similar watering method for your tomatoes, do so in the morning to allow the plant ample time to dry during the day. Choosing to stake rather than cage your tomato plants and ensuring proper spacing is advisable. This arrangement makes it a bit more challenging for diseases to propagate rapidly, and the enhanced airflow helps keep the plants dry. Regularly inspect your garden, removing any leaves exhibiting disease symptoms and eliminating infected plants.

Certain fungicides can be highly effective, but it's crucial to adhere to the instructions on the label. Using a fungicide designed for different plants, not vegetables, won't yield results and might lead to complications. For those practicing organic gardening, incorporating compost extracts or teas can serve as a treatment. To formulate a solution that prevents and addresses diseases, combine a generous tablespoon of baking soda, a teaspoon of vegetable oil, and a small quantity of mild soap with a gallon of water. Apply this solution by spraying it on the tomato plants, and be sure to reapply regularly for sustained efficacy. Prioritizing garden cleanup is another essential preventive measure, as the spores of diseases can persist on plants left in the garden from the preceding year.

Tomato Leaf Spray

Tomato leaf spray proves efficient in eradicating aphids and mites. The mechanism behind its effectiveness lies in the alkaloids present in tomato leaves (and, in fact, in the leaves of all nightshades), which are lethal to numerous insects. Just immerse 2 cups (473 milliliters) of finely chopped tomato leaves in 2 cups of water overnight. Filter the liquid the following day, discarding the leaves. Supplement the mixture with an additional 2 cups of water and apply the spray to your plants.

Garlic Oil Spray

Garlic oil spray serves as an excellent and safe insect repellent. Simply place three to four minced garlic cloves into 2 teaspoons (10 milliliters) of mineral oil. Allow the mixture to sit overnight, then strain out the garlic from the oil. Combine the oil with 1 pint (473 milliliters) of water and incorporate 1 teaspoon (5 milliliters) of environmentally friendly dish soap. Keep the solution in a bottle or jar and, when using, dilute by adding 2 tablespoons (30 milliliters) of your garlic oil mixture to one pint of water.

This blend is effective due to the presence of compounds in garlic, specifically diallyl disulfide and diallyl trisulfide, which prove irritating or fatal to certain pests, predominantly insects. The inclusion of oil and soap aids in adhering the mixture to plant leaves. Which insects does garlic oil deter? Whiteflies, aphids, and the majority of beetles will steer clear of plants treated with garlic oil.

Avoid applying this spray on a sunny day, as the oils may lead to foliage burning.

Hot Pepper Spray

Hot pepper spray proves effective for mite issues. Mix 2 tablespoons of hot pepper sauce, a few drops of eco-friendly dish soap, and 1 quart (0.94 liters) of water, allowing it to sit overnight. Apply the spray to infested plants using a spray bottle.

The efficacy of hot pepper spray stems from the presence of capsaicin, the compound responsible for the "heat" in hot peppers, which proves as irritating to insects as it is to humans (especially if you've ever experienced the sting from hot pepper in an open cut). This mixture also serves as a deterrent for whiteflies, although reapplication may be necessary if mites or whiteflies make a return.

Soap Spray

Basic soap spray effectively eliminates various prevalent household pests, such as aphids, scale, mites, and thrips. Mix 1 tablespoon of dishwashing soap with 1 gallon of water, then spray the solution on the pests.

The reliability of this approach stems from the soap dissolving the outer coating or shell of the insects, leading to their eventual demise.

Beer

Embed a tuna can or pie plate in the ground and pour a few inches of beer, stopping about 1 inch (2.5 centimeters) below the container's top. Beer is effective because slugs are drawn to the yeast.

Crucially, submerge the container into the soil, maintaining the beer approximately an inch below the soil level. This forces the slugs to descend for the beer, leading to drowning.

Citrus Rinds as Slug Traps

If you lack beer at home but have oranges, grapefruits, or lemons, experiment with this alternative. Skip the spray preparation altogether — just position the citrus peels on the ground and gather the slugs they entice.

Newspaper Earwig Traps

Newspaper earwig traps effectively diminish the numbers of these occasionally troublesome insects. Simply roll up a newspaper, fasten it with a rubber band, dampen it in water, and place it in the garden between problematic plants. Inspect the trap daily and immerse the newspaper rolls in a bucket of water to eliminate the bugs.

Cinnamon or Cayenne Pepper

Sprinkling ground cinnamon or cayenne pepper around your plants serves as a repellent, deterring ants without causing harm. This method is equally effective in maintaining a home free of bugs.

Red Pepper Spray

Red pepper spray is effective in deterring mammal and bird pests, making your plants less appealing to them. If your garden is regularly disturbed by bunnies, deer, mice, squirrels, and birds, prepare the following mixture and spray targeted plants on a weekly basis.

Combine 4 tablespoons (59 milliliters) of Tabasco sauce, 1 quart (0.94 liters) of water, and 1 teaspoon (5 milliliters) of dish soap. The capsaicin in the pepper spray will agitate the animal pests, prompting them to seek less pungent options elsewhere. Moreover, it is a safer deterrent than pesticides, reducing the risk of harm to mammals.

Baking Soda Spra

A solution with baking soda proves to be a reliable technique for warding off powdery mildew. Weekly application is essential, but if mildew troubles your garden, investing time in this method will be worthwhile. Just blend 1 tablespoon (14.7 milliliters) of baking soda, 1 tablespoon of vegetable oil, 1 tablespoon of dish soap, and 1 gallon (3.78 liters) of water. Apply the mixture by spraying it onto the foliage of plants susceptible to mildew.

Milk

Prepare a spray of 40 percent milk and 60 percent water, and apply it to both sides of the leaves on affected plants. Milk is as effective as harmful fungicides in preventing powdery mildew. Regular reapplication of this mixture is necessary, but its efficacy is impressive.

Vinegar

Vinegar is highly effective in eliminating weeds from your lawn and garden. However, it poses a risk to other plants. Employ a foam paintbrush to carefully apply vinegar directly onto the leaves of targeted weeds. This method prevents vinegar from coming into contact with other plants and guarantees thorough coverage of the entire leaf surface.

Boiling Water

Heat water to boiling and pour it over weeds in the crevices of your sidewalks or driveways. The majority of weeds can't endure this treatment, providing a solution to your issue. Exercise caution while pouring.

Vinegar and Salt

Apply boiling water to sidewalk weeds or manually pull them. For particularly resilient weeds, experiment with a mixture of 1 gallon (3.78 liters) of white vinegar, 1 cup (236 milliliters) of salt, and 1 tablespoon (14.7 milliliters) of dishwasher soap. Ensure the soap is included in the solution to prevent it from simply running off the surface of the weeds. It's important to note that this blend will eliminate almost any plant it touches, so be cautious to keep it away from your other plants and lawn.

Interestingly enough, you can grow some companion plants with your tomatoes that can act as a natural remedy to pests and diseases. Let's learn.

COMPANIONS TO PLANT WITH YOUR TOMATOES

Companion planting involves cultivating plants in close proximity in your garden to facilitate mutual benefits. These advantages can range from repelling pests to promoting plant growth and vegetable production, attracting beneficial insects and pollinators, or preventing diseases.

As an example, basil has the capability to conceal the fragrance of tomatoes from thrips, a prevalent pest affecting tomato plants. Interspersing basil plants with tomatoes can serve as a safeguard, shielding your tomato plants from thrips-induced issues like stunted growth and premature fruit drop.

Engaging in companion planting is an effortless way to alleviate pest pressure in your garden, and it can also enhance flavor and production. Simply place specific plants in close proximity to each other in the garden and witness the positive effects unfold.

You have numerous options for companion planting alongside your tomatoes, but here are the two best choices.

Basil stands out as perhaps the MOST outstanding companion plant for tomatoes. The potent aroma of basil can conceal tomatoes from various pests such as thrips, aphids, and spider mites, providing protection to the plants. Basil is also effective in deterring tomato hornworms and armyworms. Tradition suggests that planting basil near tomatoes can enhance the flavor of the tomatoes. It also contributes to efficient garden design, as tomatoes and basil are frequently used together in summer cooking.

Marigold. Beyond being a visually pleasing addition to your garden, marigolds, with their robust fragrance, serve to bewilder insects, making it challenging for them to locate your tomatoes. Additionally, these exquisite flowers excel at drawing in beneficial insects, including pollinators.

Tomatoes rank among the most favored vegetables in the garden, and even a compact home garden can gain advantages from engaging in companion planting with tomatoes!

Here is a list of some of the most effective companion plants for tomatoes:

Herbs and Blossoms
Borage
Calendula
Lemon Balm
Mint
Nasturtium
Sage
Oregano
Parsley
Thyme
Beans and peas
Carrots
Beets
Radishes
Cucumber
Squash
lettuce
Onion (Johnston 2022b)

Just like there are good companions to tomatoes, there are bad companion plants for tomatoes.

Try not to grow these plants with tomatoes to lower the number of challenges for tomato cultivation:

> Broccoli
> Cabbage
> Brussel sprouts
> Kohlrabi
> Cauliflour
> Eggplant
> Peppers
> Potaoes
> Fennel

Tomato disease codes

Many tomato varieties have been selectively bred for disease resistance. The letters appended to their names serve as codes indicating the specific diseases and insects these tomato plants are engineered to withstand.

> V - Verticillium wilt
> F - Fusarium wilt
> FF - Fusarium wilt races 1 and 2
> FFF - Fusarium wilt races 1, 2, and 3
> N - Nematodes
> A - Alternaria alternata (stem canker
> or early blight)
> T - Tobacco mosaic virus

St - Stemphylium (gray leaf spot)
TSWV - Tomato spotted wilt virus

For example, the Big Beef VFFNTA Hybrid label shows that this variety is resistant to verticillium wilt, fusarium wilt races 1 and 2, nematodes, tobacco mosaic virus, and Alternaria, and early blight.

After combating the pests and diseases you'll get happy and healthy tomato plants.

Harvesting your homegrown food is another thing that you would think is relatively simple but a common mistake that many make is to leave their tomatoes in the hope that they grow that little bit bigger and before you know it, they have gone to waste. After harvesting the perfect tomato, the next chapter will also guide you through different storage techniques.

Conclusion

In this comprehensive guide, you embarked on a journey to unlock the secrets of successful tomato cultivation. Beginning with an appreciation of the humble tomato's history, we explored the benefits of growing your own, delving into various types and their basic needs. Discovering the vast array of tomato varieties and the art of seed harvesting took us a step closer to becoming self-sufficient gardeners. As you eagerly awaited your tomato sprouts, we covered optimal planting conditions for the highest germination rates.

Understanding your tomato plant's language led us to a deep dive into soil science in "What Your Tomato Plant is Telling You About the Soil." Unraveling the mysteries of soil pH and navigating the world of fertilizers, especially organic options, empowered you to provide the ideal soil environment.

"The Fine Art of Watering Tomato Plants" emphasized the critical role water plays in plant health, exploring various irrigation methods and addressing signs of over or underwatering. To support robust growth, we explored techniques such as trellising and pruning in "Techniques to Support Tomato Plant Growth."

Navigating potential threats, "How to Protect Tomato Plants from Pests and Diseases" highlighted organic solutions, recognizing the importance of accurate identification. As we approached harvest time in "Choosing the Best Moment to Harvest Your Tomatoes and Store Them," you learned the art of optimal harvesting for flavor and nutrition, along with safe storage practices.

"You Can Grow Tomatoes Anywhere" dismantled geographical barriers, offering insights into growing tomatoes in diverse climates, containers, greenhouses, and hydroponic systems. Finally, in "Overcoming Troubles with Your Tomatoes," we shifted our focus to environmental stressors, advocating a preventative approach.

After gaining the essential tools and knowledge, it's time for you to start planting your tomatoes and get a beautiful, bright, and luscious tomato garden. Once you start cultivating your own tomatoes, your love for tomatoes will keep increasing, and the sight of your fruits will motivate you to do better and better.

All the best for your journey, and have a tomato-stic time (ouch) growing your fruits. If you learned something from this book, please leave a review.

Happy gardening!

Please Leave a Review

Now that you've got the tomato bug, you'll never look back... and you have the opportunity to ignite someone else's passion.

LET'S HEAR WHAT YOU THINK!

By leaving your honest opinion of this book on Amazon, you'll help other new gardeners find the guidance they need to succeed.

Thank you for your support. Fresh, homegrown tomatoes should be accessible to everyone – and together, we can make sure that happens.

By leaving a review of this book on Amazon, you can prevent that from happening and show other readers that this is a trusted resource.

bit.ly/3VqePiV

Percy Sargeant

Percy Sargeant grew up in the countryside of England, where the 'country garden' wasn't just a figure of speech. The formal English garden consisted of wide paths bordered with deep yew hedges and glorious displays of flowers; roses, delphiniums, foxgloves, rhododendrons, lupins, statues, and structures with climbing honeysuckle, goldfish ponds, terraces, and lavishly planted pots. Traditional and timeless elements included lawns, an area for growing vegetables, a glass greenhouse, furniture, an orchard, and some topiary.

Percy and his family moved to the United States many years ago. He observed many English-style gardens all over the country, some more English than in England, in places like Chicago, Seattle, and Denver, displaying local botany species.

When he was a young lad, with his sister and their adventurous parents, they traveled to East Africa. They lived close to the Muhesi Game Reserve in Tanzania, their home becoming a menagerie of animal pets, which included a pair of Dalmatian dogs, a few ducks, a donkey, a beehive, and a local nocturnal primate with enormous eyes called a Galago, also known as a bush baby. Under these circumstances, as a child, Percy became fascinated by the natural world and the behavior of animals. His family moved back to the countryside of England, where they set up aviaries of exotic birds alongside dogs, cats, tortoises, and a variety of other creatures. And, of course, glorious plants, a greenhouse filled with the most exquisite orchids,

Percy had studied Botany and Zoology, the investigation of plants and animals. He was fascinated by the macro world of insects. As a child, he would collect insects to observe their behavior, and not once did he stab them through the abdomen to become mounted specimens. From this experience, he learned much about the need for patience, the inevitability of failure, and the preservation of life. He would go on to capture on film the behavior of insects and larger creatures, such as exotic birds, the grizzly bear, and many other species in between. His award-winning films were subsequently shown to countless audiences across the globe. Through these times, he became acutely aware of ecology and the need to preserve life and the environment.

His fascination with plants led to his involvement in nurturing garden crops and flowers in his California home and garden, growing tomatoes, beans, radishes, beets, and much more.

Percy, these days, based on his world experience, enjoys writing about plants to let others learn and experience the many rewards of growing plants of their own.

Percy has learned over the years to maintain a high level of respect for others, including the human species, and to maintain a good sense of humor a lot of the time!

If you enjoyed this book, you may want to read my first book, which is all about growing a vegetable garden.

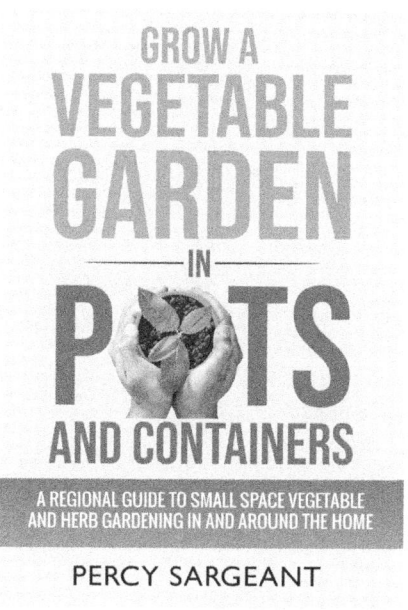

https://amzn.to/3ORQPBT

amzn.to/4aQjzCB

Acknowledgements

Waterworth, K. (2021, March 25). Puffiness in tomatoes: Why tomatoes are hollow inside. Gardeningknowhow.
https://www.gardeningknowhow.com/edible/vegetables/tomato/tomatoes-hollow-inside.htm

Hutchinson, S. (2022, October 27). Tomato leaves curling: common causes and what to do. GardenDesign.com.
https://www.gardendesign.com/tomato/leaves-curling.html

Anonymous. (2019, January 28). Tomato, cat facing. Center for Agriculture, Food, and the Environment.
https://ag.umass.edu/vegetable/fact-sheets/tomato-cat-facing

Hailey, L. (2023, October 6). 7 Reasons Your Tomatoes Aren't Setting Fruit This Season. Epic Gardening.
https://www.epicgardening.com/tomatoes-not-setting-fruit/

Sunscald of tomato and peppers. (n.d.)
https://www.missouribotanicalgarden.org/gardens-gardening/your-garden/help-for-the-home-gardener/advice-tips-resources/pests-and-problems/environmental/sunscald/sunscald-of-tomato-and-peppers

Glen, C. (n.d.). What causes tomatoes to crack? N.C. Cooperative Extension.
https://pender.ces.ncsu.edu/2020/03/what-causes-tomatoes-to-crack/

Iannotti, M. (2021, February 23). Tomato blossom drop. The Spruce.
https://www.thespruce.com/tomato-blossom-drop-1402964

A history of tomatoes. (n.d.). The University of Vermont.

https://www.uvm.edu/news/extension/history-tomatoes

Eschner, K. (2017, May 3). Tomatoes have legally been vegetables since 1893. Smithsonian Maga

zine.

https://www.smithsonianmag.com/smart-news/even-supreme-court-maintains-tomato-vegetable

-180963133/

Ld, A. H. R. (2018, October 17). Is a tomato a fruit or a vegetable? Healthline.

https://www.healthline.com/nutrition/is-tomato-a-fruit#fruits-vs-veggies

Dione, M. M., Djouaka, R., Mbokou, S. F., Ilboudo, G. S., Ouedraogo, A. A., Dinede, G., Roesel,

K., Grace, D., & Knight-Jones, T. J. (2023). Detection and quantification of pesticide residues in

tomatoes sold in urban markets of Ouagadougou, Burkina Faso. Frontiers in Sustainable Food

Systems, 7.

https://doi.org/10.3389/fsufs.2023.1213085

Chicago Health & By Cynthia Sass, MPH, RD, health.com. (2023, July 25). 7 Surprising health

benefits of tomatoes - Chicago Health. Chicago Health.

https://chicagohealthonline.com/7-health-benefits-of-tomatoes/

Hybrid Tomatoes | Varieties | California SummerWinds. (n.d.). SummerWinds Nursery.

https://www.summerwindsnursery.com/ca/plants/edibles/tomatoes/hybrid/

Fincher, M. (2021, April 27). What are heirloom tomatoes? Allrecipes.

https://www.allrecipes.com/article/what-are-heirloom-tomatoes/

In regards to tomatoes, what is meant by the terms determinate and indeterminate? (n.d.). Horti

culture and Home Pest News.

https://hortnews.extension.iastate.edu/faq/regards-tomatoes-what-meant-terms-determinate-an

d-indeterminate#:~:text=Determinate%20tomatoes%20are%20small%2C%20compact,them%20g

ood%20choices%20for%20canning

olmedaorigenes. (2022, July 1). Worldwide tomato shortage: what causes it and how can we tackle it? Olmeda Orígenes.
https://www.olmedaorigenes.com/worldwide-tomato-shortage-what-causes-it-and-how-can-we-tackle-it-2/

Consumption: 2021 in the wake of 2020 - Tomato News. (n.d.)
https://www.tomatonews.com/en/consumption-2021-in-the-wake-of-2020_2_1618.html

Fornari, C. (n.d.). The Tomato Code. GardenLady.com
https://gardenlady.com/read-articles/the-tomato-code/

How to Prepare and Store Seeds from your Tomato Plants. (2015, September 11). GrowVeg.
https://www.growveg.com/guides/how-to-prepare-and-store-seeds-from-your-tomato-plants/

Geek, T. (2023, April 7). The best places to buy tomato seeds online. Tomato Geek.
https://tomatogeek.com/where-to-buy-tomato-seeds/

Kring, L. (2023, August 3). 17 of the Best Cherry Tomatoes to Plant in Your Garden. Gardener's Path.
https://gardenerspath.com/plants/vegetables/best-cherry-tomatoes/

Emma @ Misfit Gardening. (2021, March 19). 15 Best paste tomatoes for canning - Misfit Gardening. Misfit Gardening.
https://misfitgardening.com/15-best-paste-tomatoes-for-canning/

MacArthur, A. (2023, April 19). The 15 best beefsteak tomatoes to grow in 2023. Food Gardening Network.
https://foodgardening.mequoda.com/daily/vegetable-gardening/the-best-beefsteak-tomatoes-to-grow/?amp

Ld, S. S. M. R. (2019, December 17). 7 popular types of tomatoes (and how to use them). Healthline.
https://www.healthline.com/nutrition/types-of-tomatoes

Albert, S., & Albert, S. (2023, May 30). How to make compost tea. Harvest to Table. https://harvesttotable.com/how_to_make_compost_tea/

Changing soil pH, soil pH adjustment, lowering soil pH. (n.d.). Grow It Organically. https://www.grow-it-organically.com/changing-soil-ph.html

How to fertilize tomatoes. (n.d.). PRO-MIX Gardening. https://www.promixgardening.com/en/tips/how-to-fertilize-tomatoes-80

Buiano, M. (2021, December 30). Consider this your complete guide to tomato fertilizer. Martha Stewart. https://www.marthastewart.com/8186350/tomato-fertilizer-tips

How to test your garden soil (And 3 DIY tests). (n.d.). Almanac.com https://www.almanac.com/content/3-simple-diy-soil-tests

Jeffers, A. ". (2023, December 1). Soil Texture Analysis "The Jar Test" | Home & Garden Information Center. Home & Garden Info Center | Clemson University, South Carolina. https://hgic.clemson.edu/factsheet/soil-texture-analysis-the-jar-test/

Godwin, C. (2013, April 25). How to harden off tomato plants. https://thecoeurdalenecoop.com/how-to-harden-off-tomato-plants/

Ly, L. (2023, April 11). How to repot tomato seedlings for bigger and better plants. Garden Betty. https://www.gardenbetty.com/how-to-repot-tomato-seedlings/

Iannotti, M. (2022, November 8). How to start tomato seeds indoors. The Spruce. https://www.thespruce.com/how-to-grow-tomatoes-from-seed-1403294

Let soil temperature guide you when planting vegetables. (2019, April 30). Life at OSU. https://today.oregonstate.edu/news/let-soil-temperature-guide-you-when-planting-

Vanderlinden, C. (2023, December 8). How to grow and care for tomatoes indoors. The Spruce. https://www.thespruce.com/growing-organic-tomatoes-indoors-2539817

Tomatoes. (n.d.). Royal Horticultural Society. https://www.rhs.org.uk/vegetables/tomatoes/grow-your-own

Woodstream, W. (2023, May 23). 23 Common tomato plant problems and how to fix them. https://www.saferbrand.com/articles/common-tomato-plant-problems-how-to-fix-them

Vanderlinden, C. (2023a, November 30). 15 homemade organic gardening sprays that actually work. HowStuffWorks. https://home.howstuffworks.com/green-living/homemade-organic-gardening-sprays.htm

Johnston, C. (2022, April 4). 12 Evidence-Based Companion plants for tomatoes. Growfully. https://growfully.com/companion-plants-for-tomatoes/

Wiley, D. (2023, April 18). 10 common tomato plant diseases that can wreck your crop. Better Homes & Gardens. https://www.bhg.com/gardening/vegetable/vegetables/tomato-plant-diseases/

Grant, A. (2023, June 30). Harvest time for tomatoes: When to pick tomatoes. Gardening knowhow. https://www.gardeningknowhow.com/edible/vegetables/tomato/harvest-time-for-tomatoes.htm

Hard, L. (2021, November 7). How to Store Tomatoes So They Stay Plump & Fresh for a Very Long Time. Food52. https://food52.com/blog/13796-how-to-keep-tomatoes-fresh-for-longer

Fry, P. (2023, March 30). How to Store Tomatoes So They Don't Get Mealy. Real Simple. https://www.realsimple.com/food-recipes/shopping-storing/food/how-to-store-tomatoes#toc-how-to-store-sliced-tomatoes

Dulaney, M. (2023, November 19). How to Store Tomatoes (with Long Term Storage Tips). wikiHow.

https://www.wikihow.com/Store-Tomatoes-(Long-Term)

Rd, S. C. (2023, August 8). How to can tomatoes the right way in just 5 steps. Better Homes & Gardens.

https://www.bhg.com/recipes/how-to/preserving-canning/canning-tomatoes/

Kellie. (2023, July 25). Easy Tomato Jam - the suburban soapbox. The Suburban Soapbox.

https://thesuburbansoapbox.com/easy-tomato-jam/#Instructions

Walker, E. (2023, November 8). Homemade canned spaghetti sauce. Favorite Family Recipes.

https://www.favfamilyrecipes.com/canned-spaghetti-sauce/

Paa, A. (2021, August 15). Fiery roasted salsa. Heartbeet Kitchen.

https://heartbeetkitchen.com/fiery-roasted-salsa/

Hutchinson, S. (2023, August 10). Your complete guide to watering tomato plants. GardenDe_ sign.com.

https://www.gardendesign.com/tomato/watering.html

Daniel. (2022, August 17). Underwatered tomatoes - 5 best signs to watch out for! Plantophiles.

https://plantophiles.com/gardening/underwatered-tomatoes/

Tomato pruning. (n.d.). Wisconsin Horticulture.

https://hort.extension.wisc.edu/articles/tomato-pruning/

Waddington, E. (2022, May 19). 38 Tomato support ideas for high yielding tomato plants. Rural Sprout.

https://www.ruralsprout.com/tomato-support-ideas/

Barth, B. (2020, May 15). How to grow your own tomatoes, Part 3: Staking, training and pruning - Modern Farmer. Modern Farmer. https://modernfarmer.com/2015/06/how-to-grow-your-own-tomatoes-part-3-staking-training-and-pruning/

Moulton, M. (2021, October 1). 10 tomato pests that will destroy your tomato plants - Tomato Bible. Tomato Bible.
https://www.tomatobible.com/tomato-pests/

Tomato plant diseases and how to stop them. (2010, July 16). USDA.
https://www.usda.gov/media/blog/2010/07/16/tomato-plant-diseases-and-how-stop-them

Vanderlinden, C. (2022, May 20). 75 Things You Can Compost, But Thought You Couldn't. HowStuffWorks.
https://home.howstuffworks.com/green-living/surprising-compost-items.htm

Prasanniya. (2023, July 8). How to grow hydroponic tomatoes for the absolute beginner? - Hydroponic way. Hydroponic Way.
https://hydroponicway.com/how-to-hydroponic-tomatoes/

Young, E. (2022, December 6). 9 DIY mini greenhouse ideas. Family Handyman.
https://www.familyhandyman.com/list/diy-mini-greenhouse-ideas/

Keating, K. (2023, October 10). The best grow lights for tomatoes — gardening, herbs, plants, and product reviews. Gardening, Herbs, Plants, and Product Reviews.
https://www.gardenerbasics.com/blog/best-grow-lights-for-tomatoes

Mentors, G. (2022, September 15). Growing tomatoes successfully despite cold temperatures and rain. Garden Mentors. https://gardenmentors.com/garden-help/grow-your-own-food/growing-tomatoes-successfully-despite-cold-temperatures-and-rain/

Best tomatoes for cold climates. (n.d.). Tomato Dirt.
https://www.tomatodirt.com/tomatoes-for-cold-climates.html

Mentors, G. (2022b, December 14). Best tomatoes to grow. Garden Mentors. https://gardenmentors.com/garden-help/grow-your-own-food/best-tomatoes-to-grow/

Tomatoes for hot dry climates. (n.d.). Tomato Dirt. https://www.tomatodirt.com/tomatoes-for-hot-dry-climates.html

Reid-StJohn, S. (2014, June 24). How to grow tomatoes in hot weather. Bonnie Plants. https://bonnieplants.com/blogs/garden-fundamentals/how-to-grow-tomatoes-in-hot-weather

Made in the USA
Las Vegas, NV
03 February 2025

17414980R00108